Nomad

Brandan Robertson's *Nomad* is one man's compelling account of moving beyond the boundaries of rigid religion, into an expansive true spirituality. Robertson's story is not just his own, but the story of a growing caravan of nomads who are discovering the beauty and complexity of faith and life in fresh ways. This book is a trustworthy companion for anyone who is seeking to discover a new way of being in the world.

Richard Rohr OFM, Founder, Center for Action and Contemplation

The thing about Brandan is he's really intelligent and he has a huge heart, but he's also fearless, and it's that alchemy that makes him such a compelling voice for the new thing that Jesus is up to in the world.

Rob Bell, author, *How To Be Here*

Brandan Robertson is a courageous young man. He has dared to climb fences and explore new territory outside the back yard of his religious background. He has discovered the gift of asking questions, and the joy that comes from seeking understanding with other seekers. In addition, he is a graceful and insightful writer, as *Nomad* makes clear. I hope this is the first of many!

Dr. Brian D. McLaren, author, *We Make The Road By Walking*

Nomad unfolds the tale of a fluid soul, of one who has found Living Water and is willing to both ride its spiritual rapids and float on its grace. With honesty and wit, and in fresh and luminous prose, Brandan Robertson invites others to embark on a healing journey toward the love of God.

Diana Butler Bass, author, *Grounded: Finding God in the World - A Spiritual Revolution*

Rarely have I read a book that has touched me more than *Nomad*. My friend Brandan has been captivated by Jesus and he yearns to explore and discover more of life and faith. He understands that radical community, authenticity, rhythm and belonging are deeply attractive to younger people and he gently challenges us to create more space for discovery and mystery in our church life. He challenges us to live the Jesus Movement values of grace, love, hope and forgiveness. However this book is not just theology; it is autobiography as Brandan earths this book in a deeply moving telling of his own story. I could hear his heartbeat as he bares his soul with us in a beautiful and vulnerable way. I laughed and I cried with him. This book is a gift to us all and I hope it is the first of many.

Canon Mark Russell, Chief Executive,
Church Army UK and Ireland

I first encountered Brandan Robertson in, appropriately, the very contemporary world of social media: Twitter and Facebook. There, his perspectives and viewpoints caught my eye and attracted attention. In that vein, this book has much to offer from his young, insightful, and gracious perspective, all honed in a life which has already experienced much. Brandan has harnessed those opportunities in pursuit of reflection and understanding and, in sharing them with us, provides a book - *Nomad* - replete and rich with food for our journey. It is nourishing and inspiring, gentle, but firm, and it is challenging and unsettling. For those of us who are interested in 'millennials', such as Brandan himself, and their approach to religion and spirituality, *Nomad* makes for intriguing reading.

The Rt Reverend Dr Paul Colton, Bishop of Cork,
Church of Ireland

Brandan Robertson's *Nomad* is a veritable travel guide for the spiritual journey toward God. In describing his own journey, he illuminates what most every Christian will experience along the way: the movement from the rigid religion of rules and beliefs to the spirituality and love-in-action of Jesus; the arrogance (and futility) of trying to go it alone and the inevitable pull toward community; and the collapse of a black-and-white view of the world, and its replacement with nuance and infinite shades of grey. It is one nomad's story, but it is also a story that belongs to all of us.

Bishop Gene Robinson
IX (Episcopal) Bishop of New Hampshire and Senior Fellow,
Center for American Progress, Washington, D.C.

Nomad captures the beauty and thrill of a faith set free from religious fundamentalism. This is a book for the spiritual orphans, for those hurt by the Church but still longing for a faith community, for those eager to love across boundaries and for the world changers. Robertson's words fill me with hope and make me excited to see what this rising generation has to offer the world.

Deborah Jian Lee, author of *Rescuing Jesus: How People of Color, Women and Queer Christians are Reclaiming Evangelicalism*

What surprises and delights me most about Brandan is his willingness to be honest and to take risks even as others counsel him to play it safe. Many have written about their faith journeys, but few are willing to be as deeply vulnerable as Brandan. In *Nomad*, Brandan refuses to speak in platitudes but goes to the heart of our human yearnings, exploring how our faith traditions can at once save us and kill us. This book is for seekers. It is for those of us longing for a faith that is bigger and greater than our religious doctrines where we can tell the truth of who we are, who we love, and can embrace each other's experiences along the way. If you have ever felt like a nomad in search of a spiritual home, this book will speak to you.

Rev. Dr. Sharon Groves, Vice-President of Partner Engagement, Auburn Theological Seminary, New York, NY

The brilliance of *Nomad* lies in Robertson's ability to be both incredibly relatable and spectacularly inspiring. It is not a guidebook of where to follow, but rather a blueprint for all people about how to pick up and pave their own path. After reading *Nomad*, it is clear that Robertson's vision for the future of the Church is one we should all aspire to: joyous, progressive, and fully alive.

Garrett Schlichte, contributing writer, *The Washington Post*

As Brandan's pastor during his teenage years into college I have witnessed his dedication to the Lord, to the ministry, and to bridge-building. He is indeed a gracist extending favour to many who would otherwise be marked as unfavourable. You may not agree with Brandan's conclusions, but you will identify with his journey as a nomad. Like Brandan, you and I have wandered and wondered as we have journeyed through the deserts of life only to find that grace abounds. Buckle up; you may experience such grace as you read this book.

Dr. David A. Anderson, author, *Gracism: The Art of Inclusion*

Nomad is a coming-of-age story that vulnerably explores the journey from childhood experience and provincial beliefs into a wild and wider world. Capturing the zeitgeist of a generation of young Christians, Brandan Robertson artfully explores the shock, confusion, wonder and hope of discovering a path with God that is dangerously alive.

Mark Scandrette, author, *Practicing the Way of Jesus*

A spiritual journey covering such a distance normally takes a lifetime. But this young nomad has already gleaned so much wisdom about community, identity, grace and 'the other' that his reflections-to-date are well worth the read. Insightful and incredibly readable storytelling.

Dr. Brad Jersak, Author, *A More Christlike God: A More Beautiful Gospel*

If you maintain a normative certainty about your faith, put *Nomad* down right now. This text will only scare you. Unafraid to brush aside stale theological constructions in his pursuit of Jesus, *Nomad* reveals Brandan Robertson to be a truly unique and radical reformer. With a strange and unusual grasp of the present and future of the church, I suggest that you read *Nomad* and anything else Robertson writes.

Rev. Dr. Jeff Hood, Baptist Pastor and Public Theologian

Brandan Robertson offers penetrating insight into the minds of a new generation of followers of Jesus – insights we all need to be interacting with. Committed to seeking out God beyond the old binaries that seem to consistently gridlock our conversations, Brandan paves the way forward for the spiritual (but not necessarily religious) to rediscover a vibrant and transformative faith while embracing the doubts and tensions that life brings.

Daniel Hill, Author, *10:10: Life to the Fullest*

Nomad

A Spirituality for Travelling Light

Brandan Robertson

First published in Great Britain in 2016 by
Darton, Longman and Todd Ltd
1 Spencer Court
140 – 142 Wandsworth High Street
London SW18 4JJ

ISBN 978-0-232-53258-6

A catalogue record for this book is available from the British Library

Phototypeset by Kerrypress, St Albans AL3 8JL
Printed and bound in Great Britain by Bell & Bain, Glasgow

Dedicated to

**Phyllis Tickle
(1934-2015)**

*Who agreed to write the foreword to this book before she passed on,
and whose love, light, wit, and intellect inspired me
to push beyond the boundaries of religion
and into the vast terrain of a vibrant spirituality.*

Contents

Introduction: An unexpected journey

When I started writing this book in the autumn of 2013, I could never have imagined the journey on which I was about to embark. At the time, I was a senior at a Christian College in Chicago, getting ready to graduate with my degree in Theology and move on to whatever God had in store for me next. Over the course of my short faith journey and especially during the course of my studies in college, my entire worldview and paradigm was turned upside down and inside out. The person I was emerging as from college seemed to be the exact opposite of the person I was when I had entered college. From being an ultra-orthodox defender of the faith, I was now being called a heretic and false teacher.

While I was in college, I began to develop an overwhelming conviction that the way the Church treated sexual and gender minorities (and many other groups as well) was deeply flawed and actually destroyed lives instead of restoring life. I watched as my friends in school were plagued with fear about their sexual orientation and how our college might react if they ever shared their 'struggle' with same-sex attraction. I met LGBT+ people around Chicago who had been kicked out of homes, forced into conversion therapy programmes, or severely abused by religious leaders because they decided to be authentic about their God-given sexuality or gender identity. And, in the midst of it all, I, for the first time, began to realise that I too 'struggled' with same-sex attraction.

As a good Evangelical Christian who felt called to be a pastor, I knew that this 'struggle' had to be kept quiet, lest I become the recipient of the harsh treatment I had seen the Church dish out to others. I quietly confessed my 'sin-struggle' to a few friends for accountability and shared it with a professor who openly shared his story about living life as an openly gay man and finding liberation from 'the lifestyle' through faith in Jesus. But because this particular sin is in fact seen as more insidious than almost any other, news of my struggle quickly spread around campus to other professors and administrators. Before I knew it, I was being called into meetings with the Dean of our college to answer questions about my 'theological fitness' and sexual struggles. During my senior year, things got particularly difficult. I was called into the office of a professor who sat me down and with rage in her eyes told me she believed I was 'demon possessed' and had 'gotten away with murder' by bringing my 'agenda' to the campus of our conservative Bible college. Still identifying as a conservative, non-LGBT+ affirming Evangelical, I looked her in the eye and assured her that she had gotten me all wrong. I told her I wanted to serve God, to love people, and to help build bridges between the Church and the world. I told her I wanted to prove I wasn't this wicked monster she perceived me as, but a faithful Christian. In order to prove that to her, she ordered me a reparative therapy text book and urged me to begin meeting with her colleague who practiced 'healing prayer', a theophostic prayer technique meant to help heal me of my 'homosexual desires'.

So I did. For the rest of my senior year, I met weekly with a professor for healing prayer. Every week I would confess all of my sins, would be anointed with holy water, and would spend an hour in deep prayer, asking God to reveal periods of abuse in my life that had contributed to my 'same-sex attractions' so that they could be healed. Over the course of the year, I did, in fact, experience tremendous healing. I felt more complete than I had for as long as I could remember. But as I worked through the trauma and wounds from my past, I discovered that my sexuality wasn't being healed at all. Only strengthened. When I finally walked across the stage to receive my Bachelor's diploma in an ornate church in downtown Chicago, I stepped into the vast unknown of the future with little sense of direction or vision for where I wanted to go. I felt deeply hurt by the intense rejection and abuse I had experienced at the hands of many professors at my college, and confused about what to believe about my own sexuality.

During that summer after graduating, I spent many weeks pouring myself into this manuscript. I relocated from Chicago to Washington, D.C., my home town, and spent days locked away in my parents' tiny apartment writing, editing, praying, crying, giving birth to this book that you now hold in your hands. I also spent countless hours studying the Bible and mounds of theological literature about homosexuality, hoping to find some clear sense of what God really wanted me to do and believe in relation to my own same-sex attractions. The more I studied and prayed, the more I sensed that the Holy Spirit was gently nudging me, telling me that all of these experiences were preparing me for something bigger than I could imagine. All of the pain, fear, humiliation, and angst was going to be redeemed, used in some way to help bring reformation and revival within the Church.

I was overwhelmed by this sense of nudging. Everything I read in Scripture and all of my experiences kept pointing me in this direction. Was I really supposed to step out on this most divisive issue? I knew that if I did, it could cost me my dreams of being an Evangelical pastor. I prayed and I wrestled until I couldn't hold it in any longer. Later that summer, the Spirit gave me the final push that I needed. A group of Evangelicals in Washington D.C. was just beginning to form that would advocate for civil marriage equality for same-sex couples among Evangelical Christians. I had begun having conversations with them, but to my surprise,

I received a call from one of the founders who asked me if I'd be interested in becoming the national spokesperson for this new effort they were calling Evangelicals for Marriage Equality. Just a year earlier, I would have never even considered taking such a position. But now, even in the midst of my theological uncertainty around homosexuality, this felt like a clear door being opened by God.

As I took the position, I was thrown into a national spotlight as one of the 'leading voices' on the topic of homosexuality and Christianity. I felt incredibly inadequate for this position and unprepared for the response that the Christian community would have for me. Within weeks of our organization's launch, Evangelical leaders like Dr Albert Mohler and Andrew Walker publicly denounced our organisation, claiming that our arguments lacked true substance and were essentially just concessions to our fallen and sinful culture. I received handwritten letters from professors at my Bible college who were 'deeply grieved' by my support for same-sex marriage and even called for me to 'renounce' my degree, claiming that I received it under 'false pretenses' as a 'deceiver'.

The pain of being rejected by some of the very people that I admired the most is one of the most unbearable situations I've ever experienced. Christian leaders who I once idolised were now publicly calling me the enemy. This rejection caused a lot of soul-searching within me, seeking to determine if I was really doing the right thing. I spent a lot of time praying and reading the Bible, and I kept being drawn back to the image of Jesus as the voice for the voiceless, the defender of the oppressed. Under no circumstances did it make sense in my mind for Christians to oppose the *civil rights* of sexual and gender minorities to have access to all the same rights and privileges that every other citizen in our country enjoyed. I didn't see how these civil rights harmed any Christian's religious freedoms or ability to defend the sacrament of marriage within their own denomination or church. I felt the Spirit of God reassuring me that I was doing the right thing. I was following the path of Jesus. And it would be a costly path to walk down, but it was, as a mentor of mine often says, what love truly required of me.

As my platform as a pro-LGBT+ Evangelical voice grew, so did questions about my own sexuality. Reporters would frequently ask if I identified as 'straight'. Initially, I said yes, but as time went on and I spent more time studying and thinking about sexuality from a Christian perspective, I slowly felt emboldened to begin using the word 'questioning' to identify my sexuality. I wasn't sure what I was. I was attracted to women, for sure, but also to men. But I also recognised the significant hurdles that would be placed in front of me if I formally identified as a sexual minority. How could I ever pastor an Evangelical church if I identified as LGBT+? I knew that any step towards 'coming out' (read, being honest) would forever end my career as an Evangelical leader.

In January of 2015, I decided to take a short break from my public ministry and go to Bermuda for a mini retreat to finish the manuscript of *Nomad*. With all of the public work that I was involved with, I had fallen behind on my deadline to complete the book and wanted to get it finished before February rolled around. I spent five days on that little British island off the eastern coast of the United States, writing, meditating, and relaxing. When I returned at the end of the month, I had finished the manuscript and sent it off to my publisher. I was so relieved. I had done it - the thing that just a few years ago seemed to be impossible. I had written an entire book. I was excited to begin the process of editing and sending it out for endorsements.

However, this excitement didn't last very long. A few hours after clicking 'send' on the email to my publisher, I received an email back. 'I'm sure it feels amazing to have the manuscript finished! Since you've been receiving more media attention over the past few months, we've had some questions/concerns arise from our buyers, and our executive team has asked that I connect with you about your stance on a few issues that may continue to come into question.' As soon as I read those words, I knew what was about to happen. My publisher, who had signed a contract with me precisely because I was 'progressive' and pushing the boundaries of Evangelicalism, was going to drop my book deal because of my public support for same-sex marriage.

After a brief phone call, my publisher sent me their doctrinal statement on 'homosexuality'. The statement consisted of a few comments and a quote from 1 Corinthians 6: 9-11, the emphasis being on the statement, 'Do not be deceived; neither fornicators, nor idolaters, nor adulterers, nor effeminate, nor homosexuals, nor thieves, nor the covetous, nor drunkards, nor revilers, nor swindlers, shall inherit the kingdom of God.' I took a deep breath and sent my response to the publisher. I told them that I could not affirm their statement or interpretation of those passages and that I understood what that meant for my book deal. Just over a week later, I received a phone call telling me that my contract had been cancelled. *Nomad* was no more.

Almost immediately the news about my book spread. *TIME* magazine ran an article entitled 'Young Evangelical Leader Loses Book Deal After Coming Out'. In that article, for the first time, I was publicly identified as 'queer', and within an hour I had received hundreds of Facebook messages and emails from friends, mentors, and family members either commending or condemning me for my decision to identify as 'queer'. The next few weeks are a blur to me. Around twenty news outlets around the world covered the story and I began receiving countless calls from publishers and authors offering their support to me in this period of loss. I was overwhelmed. After talking to a number of mentors, I decided that it was best for me to take step back to talk with family and friends who had just read the news about my 'queer' sexual identity and to think about what the next steps would be for my book and public ministry.

The spring of 2015 was a rough season for me. But it was also a season of tremendous growth. Out of the pain and disorientation, a mirror was held up to my life and I was able to take a good, hard look at the path I was walking. In this season, I felt more sure than ever that 'coming out', even if it wasn't in the ideal manner, was one of the best things to have happened to me. Because although I received a ton of hate mail from old college professors, former Christian friends, and strangers warning me of the 'dangerous path' I was walking down, I also experienced more love, support, and freedom in my life than I'd ever had before. I was hiding nothing. I was standing firm in my God-created identity and I felt more in step with the Spirit of God than I had in a long time. I began attending an open and affirming Evangelical church in the heart of Washington, D.C. and began to get connected to a new community that embraced me and celebrated me. By the time the summer came, my life had gone from being dark and filled with fear to bright and whole.

I was reminded of the Scripture from Psalm 30:5, that proclaims, 'Though the sorrow may last for the night, joy comes with the morning'. Though I had felt the sharp sting of rebuke and rejection and had lost the book that I had spent so much time working on, my life continued to move forward. The cost of being 'outed' and losing a book deal seemed well worth the liberation and life that I stepped into. I had never expected to become a 'poster child' for LGBT+ Christians, but it seemed that life had very different plans. I knew that I was called by God to be a pastor and through these difficult circumstances; God provided a platform for that to happen in a unique way. I began receiving messages, emails, and phone calls from closeted LGBT+ Christians who were inspired by my story and sought me out for prayer and guidance. I began meeting with Evangelical pastors who felt guilty for the way the Church had treated me and many other sexual and gender minorities and wanted my help speaking out against this discriminatory behavior. I began to see firsthand that the Spirit of God was truly up to something unbelievable in the Church, and it wasn't coming from the centres of power, but from the margins. God was beginning a revival, it seemed, through sexual and gender minorities, and God had made me a part of this amazing movement. We still have a lot of work to do and a long way to go. But God is doing a new thing in our midst, and this renewal movement cannot be stopped. I was, and continue to be, in awe of the amazing honour to be one voice in a growing chorus of Christians speaking up as, and on behalf of, sexual and gender minorities in the Church today.

So, what happened to the book? Well, quite obviously, it got published. In the winter of 2015-16, while working on another manuscript for my next book, I was nudged by a publisher in the United Kingdom about *Nomad*. I had been holding onto the book for a while, waiting until the right moment to begin showing it around again, but when the email came through from DLT, something felt *right*. After a series of conversations between the editors at DLT and my literary agent, we signed a contract and planned a tour to the United Kingdom and Ireland in the summer of 2016 to release the book you now hold in your hand. It was quite peculiar for me to have my book first published in the United Kingdom and Ireland before North America, but it turns out that it was just the way it was meant to be. Through the process of publishing with DLT, I have been afforded the great opportunity to be connected to, learn from, and collaborate with so many amazing people of faith across the United Kingdom and beyond who have been working hard to secure the place of sexual and gender minorities at the table of grace. More than that, I have discovered that there is a whole caravan of people throughout the UK and Ireland who are walking and have walked this nomad journey. I have been so inspired and blessed by these fellow sojourners and am so thrilled to share this book with them first.

The book you hold in your hand is not primarily about sexuality or gender identity. Instead, it's about my journey so far from the rigid confines of religion to the vast desert sands of true spirituality. And though the book is about my story, I really believe that it's about *all* of our stories. We're *all* on the nomad's journey and *all* are living life step by step, wondering as we wander, experiencing the crazy, painful, joyous reality that we call life. It is my sincerest hope that you will allow me to be a companion with you along your journey as you read the words of this book, as we trek forward towards life beyond limits.

Thank you for picking up this book and embarking on this journey with me. May the Spirit of God be our guide.

Let's begin.

1

Nomad

*There is stability in walking an uncertain path,
because you never allow yourself to be misled
by what you think you know.*

A.J. Darkholme

Imagine massive, golden deserts. In the midst of the eternal sands, a lowly man rides high atop a camel, dusty winds blowing around him in every direction. The camel slouches under the weight of the nomad's bags, filled with treasures and mementos the wanderer has acquired in his travels. As the camel lifts each hoof to place it down again, the track immediately behind it disappears as the sand fills it back in. They leave no record of where they came from, no trail to suggest in which direction they are heading.

Yes, their journey is seasoned with guidance from other travellers who have crossed these same landscapes. But there is no one set of footprints to follow—step by step, their path is uniquely their own.

A lonely sojourn, perhaps. But I see the man as curious and optimistic—roaming the dunes, relying only on his instinct and the wind to guide him. No destination is final, because he is never satisfied with where he is, and he is always ready to embark on a new quest to find a place that feels a little bit more like home.

I am that nomad. My life has been filled with wandering through the vast expanse of reality, searching for a place I can call home. Or in laypeople's terms, I'm a spiritually discontented, ADD millennial. For as long as I can remember, I have been fascinated with the big questions about life. I don't expect that one day I will arrive at 'the answers' and quit asking the questions. Yes, I want insights—but they will enable me to ask these same questions in different ways, perhaps with more life wisdom to illuminate them.

I grew up surrounded by kids who came from different cultures and religions, each with their own unique set of practices, rituals, and answers to the questions I was asking. This diversity was not confusing; it was stimulating. In elementary school, my best friend Augusto and I would sit on a bench during recess and have deep conversations about the purpose of our lives. In middle school, I began engaging in even deeper conversations about faith with my Muslim and atheist friends. After I had a radical conversion to Christianity at the age of twelve, I continued to explore, debate, and seek out answers beyond the ones I was hearing at my Baptist church.

I have spent the last decade of my life as an Evangelical Christian, recently graduating from a Bible college with a degree in Pastoral Ministry and Theology. You'd think that my wanderings would have begun settling down by now. Certainly the expectations of my academic institution were to establish my foundations in the worldview they affirmed. I started an interview-based radio show designed to help us learn from those with whom we disagreed, but it was cancelled when the discussions roamed too far afield of acceptable worldview boundaries. The priorities seemed to be more about forging and affirming the right convictions than questioning them.

In contrast, I have found that the deeper I grow in my own faith as a Christian, the greater my desire to explore. Not because of the 'inadequacy' of Christianity to give meaning to my life or to connect me to God, but quite the opposite. I have found a relationship with God through my faith in Jesus. Yet I have also discovered that the purpose of my faith is *not* to provide all of the answers. Jesus didn't come so that his disciples would comprehend all of the mysteries of God and life. My Christian faith instead has served as the lens through which I see the world and the pattern in which to model my life. Christ liberates us to explore. To seek and to find. To knock on doors and discover what may lie behind them.

My faith doesn't end my search; it inspires it. It amps up my curiosity and whets my appetite for discovering what God is doing in and through the world each and every day. I have a spirituality that travels; it is always on the move. Yes, I have convictions, but they are treasures in my nomad's bag. Travelling light gives me a way to set down what would otherwise be the baggage of someone else's decision to cling to a well-worn path.

I realise this approach is out of step with a religious culture that tends to value certainty over curiosity. Christians often define themselves by what they believe versus what others don't. There is security in staying in a particular place with people who share our convictions and experiences. And there is nothing wrong with that, but it's not a one-size-fits-all way of faith. For a growing number of us, this way of having faith is simply unrealistic and inconceivable. We need to move. We want to push the boundaries and traverse in lands where no one has gone before. We're nomads.

This book is a chronicle of some of the most important lessons I have learned thus far along my journey of faith. I have set out to write it not because I believe I have some superior knowledge to impart or anything particularly innovative to say. Instead, I write to encourage my fellow nomads who, like me, so often feel alone in their wanderings. I hope to remind that you are a part of a much larger caravan of fellow wanderers who are seeking to discover for ourselves the meaning and mysteries of life. If any of my ramblings and reflections resonate with you, perhaps you will find yet another sojourner on your journey.

But I also write for those who are *not* particularly interested in the life of wandering. Those who prefer a much more organised and systematised spirituality and find those of us with spiritual ADD absolutely maddening. For you, I hope to help flesh out the thought processes and spiritual inclinations of a growing number of people so that in getting a glimpse into the mind of one of us, you might better understand others.

I believe that our universe is truly enchanted, filled with the Spirit of an indescribable and grandiose God, whose height, breadth, width, and depth can never be comprehended. So no matter who you are holding this book, I pray that its whirlwind of thoughts and words might fan the flame of your faith and kindle your inner sense of wonder. May your desire to trek further into the uncharted territories of God be intensified, and may you find the courage you need to take the next step of your journey - maybe here and now, with me.

2

Wander

Not all those who wander are lost.
J.R.R. Tolkien, *The Lord of the Rings*

Have you ever wandered off and realised that you had no idea where you were? The wide range of emotions you experience when you realise that you're lost is fascinating. Depending on where you're lost or the circumstances leading up to your disorientation, you might have a sense of excitement. Adrenaline begins to pump as you consider all of the opportunities you have to explore your unfamiliar surroundings. Other times, discovering that you're lost can lead to sheer terror. Like the time you were walking through the shopping mall with your mom and you walked by the toy store. After locking eyes with the new X-Man action figure, you turn around to realise that your mom has continued walking and is no longer in front of you and you're surrounded by a crowd of people you don't know. In that moment, a palpable sense of terror overcomes you and you do the only thing you know to do – cry. Loudly. Hoping that your mom hears the familiar noise and comes back to rescue her child from his treacherous circumstances. No matter what the situation, wandering off and getting lost are an unavoidable part of our lives.

And personally, I kind of like it. When I was learning to drive, my mom absolutely hated getting in the car with me. Not because I was a bad driver (at least not in *my* opinion), but because a car ride was never just a car ride with me. If we were driving to the grocery store, I would always end up turning down a random street to discover where it led. I love to get behind the wheel and roam all over God's creation. I cannot tell you how many times I have ended up discovering curious new places that I never knew existed by simply wandering around.

One of my favourite wandering experiences was just a few years ago when I was on a road trip with my friend Troy to a festival in North Carolina. We had been camping out in the foothills of the Smoky Mountains. One day when Troy had gone to grab lunch across the campground, I had the awesome idea to hop in his car and go for a quick spin. So, without giving it another thought, I grabbed the keys and took off up the remote mountain highway. After driving for about twenty minutes, I came to the most stunning rest area that overlooked the historic mountain towns in the valley beneath. For the next hour, I sat at the overlook gazing at the splatters of colour that dotted the horizon around me. I was awestruck.

My mountaintop experience quickly came to an end as my cell phone began to ring. It was Troy wondering where in the heck I had taken his car. I couldn't believe his audacity – calling me and interrupting this sacred moment! After he hung up, I took one last survey of the magnificent work of divine art and reluctantly got back in the car and made my way back down the mountain to our campsite.

These are the sorts of experiences that we would never get to have if we were not willing to wander off the beaten path every now and then. For me, it's almost a compulsive tendency. I love exploration and the sense of adventure that comes with deviating from a set course of action. Some may see this as a weakness. Others may diagnose it as ADD. I, on the other hand, have come to embrace it as a gift. It's because of my propensity to meander that I continually have new opportunities to find and be found. Allowing myself to wander off into the vast jungles of religion and spirituality has often led to me stumbling upon life altering new ways of thinking, living, and being.

What's really ironic, however, is that along with the gift of wandering, I have long sensed a calling from God to be a Pastor – a spiritual shepherd of sorts. (God really does have a sense of humour!) How could these two giftings fit together? Actually, I have discovered, quite well. Too often in Christianity we equate wandering with negative categories like eternal damnation, deception, and going 'astray'. We have often stigmatised those who wander from our group as weak and easily deceived. But what if we've been wrong? What if one's tendency to go wandering off is truly a gift? What if the driving force beneath the curiosity that leads a person to wander off the beaten path is not immaturity, but the wild, untamable Spirit of God, drawing them into the foliage to be refined, to discover fresh insights, and pioneer a new way forward for a new group of people?

In my disorientation, I have been forced to attune myself to the gentle breeze of God's Spirit and allow myself to be moved into new, unexplored territories. Sure, it's scary sometimes. Uncomfortable most of the time. But it's always rewarding.

Many who watch my spiritual journey from a distance have consigned me to the category of 'lost', as if that were a bad thing. But it's only when we allow ourselves to get lost that we can have the opportunity to find and be found. Many people in our churches take great pride in the fact that they've been 'found' by God and firmly plant their feet into the ground, refusing to move. We often look at those people, the unmovable pillars of our community, as valiant and honourable. We admire their lack of questions and uncertainty a wise and desirable. Many of us desperately seek to be people who 'stand firm', which really just means pretend we know it all because, if we're honest, we know that no one who *thinks* they've got life figured out *actually* has *anything* figured out. Many people spend their lives gripping on to the certainty and satisfaction of being among the 'found' ones and miss out on the vast world of possibilities that there is to explore.

Being confident in one's faith is not a bad thing. That's not at all what I am suggesting. But what I am saying is that those who are the *most* confident are often those who don't have any fun. They're the ones who stay in the backyard, just like mom told them, instead of going to explore the make-believe lands on the other side of the fence. If they're not willing to explore beyond the realm of their safety, certainty, and comfort, they will never know if their fantasies are true.

In our increasingly interconnected world (thanks to social media), more and more people are discovering the thrill of exploring the wide array of ideas, beliefs, practices, doctrines, and spiritualities that exist within our world. Many people are leaving the safe confines of the faith of their upbringing and are roaming the streets, looking for and often discovering, new and innovative ways of expressing their devotion to God. This isn't a symptom of unfaithfulness but is, I believe, a movement of God's Spirit. As a new generation of Christians are taking to the streets of the world, looking for signs of God's movement in the most unlikely and unexpected places, we are discovering that the God we worship is much bigger than we once expected. That Jesus is actually 'alive and active' as the Apostle Paul says in the book of Ephesians, in places we never thought he would show up.

Too often in Christian contexts we talk about God and our faith in him as if we have it all figured out. We value certainty and clarity. We can quickly name off a list of attributes that describe who we believe God to be: omnipotent, sovereign, omnipresent, holy, righteous, just, and so on. We profess our beliefs about God and life with boldness, believing that we have arrived at an understanding of capital 'T' Truth that no one can deny. You've been there, haven't you? I spent a good number of years in this space and it was a great place to be. Life seemed to be so clear. My direction was certain. My beliefs were settled. The Bible said it, I believed it, and that settled it.

This worked well for me for some time. But then, life happened.

It doesn't take much to shake up the snow globe of our lives a make everything that once seemed so clear incredibly blurry. Relationships. Family drama. Doubts. Conflicts. Questions. Growth. Change. Pain. And it's in the dust up of life's circumstances that we often find ourselves stumbling off the path that was set before us and by the time the dust begins to settle, we find out that we're not in Kansas anymore. The things we once thought we knew are now in question. The way we thought life worked no longer proves to be true. These times of disillusionment are both terrifying and exhilarating. On one hand, we get to explore and experience life in fresh ways. On the other hand, nothing makes sense anymore. We begin to find some of things we were taught about God to be questionable at best, or else downright untrue. This not only can lead us to spiritual vertigo, but also a great amount of pain and distrust for the people, systems, and structures that failed to prepare us for the reality of life.

What are we supposed to do when our faith seems to fail us? When our religion runs counter to the reality that we experience in everyday life? What happens when the pat answers that once made so much sense now begin to seem uneducated, ill informed, and archaic? What are we to do when we seem to grow out of God? Or at least the understanding of God that we grew up with?

It's questions like these that have led me to write this book. The Christian world is filled with books, blogs, and curriculums that claim to walk with us through the 'difficult questions'. They seek to help defend a particular version of the faith. They have a destination in mind from the start. I have been through most of those books. I have read most of those blogs. I have studied the curriculums. But through it all, I have discovered that what I am seeking is not answers to my questions. I have come to believe that questions of this magnitude can probably never be definitively answered. That why humans continue to ask the same questions over and over again in every generation. We've never really found the answers, despite the claims and convictions of many religious groups.

Instead of answers, what I have often yearned for more than anything are for companions in my wondering, those who would be open and honest with their thoughts, struggles, and experiences, and wouldn't be afraid to delve deep into the mysteries of faith and life with me. Over the years, I have been blessed to have had many such friends in my life. But even still, I have often felt like a stranger. Like I was the only one who spent more time asking questions than seeking answers. Like I was the only one who didn't quite fit in with anybody in my church. Like I was the only one who felt like a sojourner in the midst of a vast crowd of people who seemed to have already found answers to the questions that continually surfaced within my heart. When I began blogging about my struggles and questions a few years ago, I was surprised to find that I wasn't alone after all. That hundreds of others around the world were experiencing the same feeling of homelessness in the Church. Many of them reached out to me weekly through my blog and we began to form a tribe of hopeful wanderers through social media.

It is my hope that this book will serve, in some degree, as a voice of empathy to all of my fellow nomads who never seem to be able to find a place to call home. I hope that this book is able to put into words some of your deepest thoughts. Not because I am especially wise or insightful, but because your thoughts have been my thoughts too. I hope that as you read this book, my words will resonate with the vagabond spirit of many in my generation.

Over the past decade as I have traversed through life as a Christian, I have come face to face with these harrowing questions and have struggled to find answers like so many other young people of faith. My story and struggles aren't unique. They aren't new. And I am certainly not pretending to be an expert theologian or spiritual teacher who has any absolute answers to these questions. Instead, I am simply one man who is trying to find my way in this wilderness that we call life.

The first time I stumbled on Jesus in an unexpected place was during my freshman year in Bible college. After growing restless in our search for a church to call home, a couple of friends and I decided that we'd go rogue and explore some faith communities that weren't listed on our school's 'Recommended Churches' list. On our first Sunday, we decided to go to a church that was just a few blocks away from our school on the same street. We had heard rumours that they had 'abandoned the Gospel' and so as we entered the old, stone church building, we were all a little nervous. No one was sure what to expect. We walked in to the colourful sanctuary and were energetically greeted by the ushers who escorted us to a pew near the front of the nearly packed sanctuary. The congregation was made up of men and women from all ages, colours, and backgrounds. In the pew behind us sat a large, African American man who was clearly homeless. In front of us, to our chagrin, was a well-dressed, middle class lesbian couple. As soon as we realised that this was one of *those* kinds of churches, we understood why our school had removed it from its list of recommendations. Surely the Spirit of God couldn't be at work in a place like this. The service began with singing a few popular Evangelical worship songs, which struck me as strange, because these people weren't supposed to be *real* Christians.

After the worship set was completed a peppy, young white woman with a big Bible approached the pulpit. This was their pastor. A *woman*. Talk about a shock to a couple of fundamentalist-leaning Bible college freshmen. She opened her Bible and began to preach from Isaiah 58 – a passage about social justice. Of course. But as we sat through the message, it became clear to me that this woman was deeply rooted in Jesus. She loved God, knew her Bible, and preached with a passion that would give any Evangelical minister a run for their money. As she concluded her sermon, my heart melted with conviction as I reflected on her message: God calls us to live the Gospel not only with our words, but in the way we treat the poor, oppressed, and marginalised. This message was rooted in the Bible. She referenced Jesus about eight times in the course of her sermon. I felt the tugging of the Spirit on my hardened heart. This was not supposed to be happening. I was *not* supposed to be sensing the Spirit of God at work in a place as theologically skewed as this. Or was I?

After the service ended, we were invited by an elderly couple sitting in the pew next to us to join them downstairs for coffee and pastries. These people seemed to have the whole 'Evangelical' thing down pat – from worship music, to preaching, to the after service food. In the basement of the church, we stuck out like sore thumbs. My friends and I were dressed in neatly pressed shirts and I was wearing a yellow tie with blue crosses patterned across the front. We had large Bibles and journals to take sermon notes in under our arms. We screamed 'Bible college students' and everyone knew it. One woman approached us and introduced herself as the associate pastor of the church. She began our conversation by saying: 'You're from Moody, aren't you?' We were proud of our vocation as Bible college students preparing for ministry. As we conversed with this pastor, we were caught off guard both by her kindness and her rootedness in Christ. She explained her journey of faith with us and her passion for being the hands and feet of Jesus to our neighbourhood and city. She encouraged us to attend the Bible study that would be taking place in just a few minutes. 'Bible study?' I thought. 'These people *study* the *Bible*?' We politely declined her offer and headed back to our campus.

As soon as we walked out of the church, my friends and I looked at each other. The colour left our faces. We were in shock. We had just had a very positive, Jesus-centred experience at a church we had been warned had abandoned the faith. We felt encouraged and even convicted by the Holy Spirit by the message the woman pastor preached. The people were so genuine. They even had a *bible study*. These realisations shook us to our core. We had been told that this church was dangerous, but what we found was a community of beautiful brothers and sisters in Christ. The Sprit of Jesus was so evident, even in a place that had significantly different theology, practices, and worldviews from us. This experience ignited a passion in my soul for exploring beyond the boundaries that I had been taught to stay within. Every Sunday for the remainder of the semester, my friends and I decided to visit a different church every week, and on almost every Sunday, we had transformative and edifying experiences in communities we had been taught to keep our distance from and even to demonise and warn others about. In other words, we continued to find Jesus hanging out in places where he wasn't supposed to be, according to our religious leaders. How very Christ-like of him.

This is the value of wandering. The value of breaking the rules and leaving the backyard, where we know we are safe, and wandering in to strange, unknown territory. Every time I have wandered in my faith, I have ended up experiencing God in fresh ways. I have come to see that exploration is not a practice of the unfaithful, but rather is exactly what being a follower of Christ is actually all about. If you have ever read through the Gospels, then you know that Jesus is always pushing his followers to move beyond their comfort zones. He led them into uncomfortable and often un-kosher (pun intended) situations. He caused them to have far more questions than answers. I believe the reason Jesus did this was because he was far more interested in allowing his disciples to cultivate a relationship and trust with and in him than leading them to a place of 'arrival'. Jesus wasn't worried about giving anyone any answers. He was interested in leading them on a journey. Jesus created spiritual nomads, not doctrinal guards. Jesus stirred up doubt in the minds of those who thought they had it all figured out and honoured the seekers. Those who sought after God had to remain humble. Those who thought they had God all figured out were oppressive and proud. I have experienced the same reality in my own journey. James, Jesus' little brother, reminds us that 'God *resists* the proud but gives grace to the humble.' (James 4:6)

It is only when we learn to value our wandering and lack of knowing and find ourselves relying on the untamable wind of

God's Spirit to guide us into uncharted waters that we receive grace and truth. Following God is about wandering down the roads less travelled and discovering the pearl of great price buried in a field. When we begin to understand this as the pattern of life that we are called to follow, our lives begin to radically change. We no longer find our identity or value in having the right theology or being a part of the right denomination. Instead, we recognise that we, along with the rest of humanity, are just sojourners in this life. Our eyes are opened and we begin to discover Jesus hanging out in unexpected places and with the most unlikely of people, all around us. Life becomes a scavenger hunt, following after the wind of God's Spirit off the beaten path, never knowing where we are heading, but trusting that wherever it is, God will be there and it's going to be amazing.

Wandering has become the foundation of my spiritual life. And the journey down each new path and into each new tribe of people is absolutely thrilling.

3

Redeemed

'Behold, I am making all things new.'
Jesus Christ

From the moment we take our first breath, we embark on this strange and exhilarating journey called life. We have little choice in the matter. From the moment we arrive into this world we are given a blank canvas that immediately begins to be spattered with the cornucopia of colours with their various tones and hues which comprise the portrait that will gradually compose our life. On one hand, we are the artists, free to create whatever we desire from the materials we have been given. On the other hand, our supplies, abilities, and the very canvas that we create upon are given to us by an untamable and imaginative Force that lies just beyond our scope of vision. That grand Virtuoso of the universe who has shaped us and placed within us the visions and dreams for the masterpiece we will one day create with this thing called life.

Contradictions have always been a fundamental part of my life. I grew up in Elkridge, Maryland, a mid-sized town squeezed tightly between Baltimore and Washington D.C., located in one of the most prestigious and wealthy counties in the country. The historic town was dotted with colonial-era mansions owned by wealthy lawyers, doctors, and politicians, with manicured lawns and private driveways leading back to the homes that sit on acres of land densely rich with tall oak trees. Many of the kids I went to school with came from the wealthy families who lived in these homes, and they were a well-dressed and privileged bunch. I, on the other hand, didn't grow up in any of these mansions. My parents weren't lawyers or doctors – my mom worked in a doctor's office as an office manager and my dad laid carpet for a living. We lived in one of two large trailer parks that were located on the edge of the town in a single-wide, 3 bedroom mobile home. Now because of the location of our trailer park, this was no ordinary, run-down neighbourhood. The 600 trailers in our development were surrounded by a forest and a small stream. There were playgrounds located throughout the neighbourhood and even a large community pool. Though most of the families that lived in our neighbourhood fit squarely into the lower-class social bracket, we tried our hardest to live as if we were equal with the neighbourhoods that surrounded us.

As I grew up, I worked hard to fit in with the rest of my peers. Thinking back, I am not sure how my parents did it, but I generally always pulled off the preppy white guy look in school, decked out in Hollister and American Eagle for as long as I can remember. Financial struggles were very real for my family while I was growing up, oftentimes living paycheck to paycheck, I often watched my parents argue and stress about paying the bills. None the less, we all got very good at blending in with our surroundings and hiding the reality of our many struggles. Constructing illusions about what my reality was like and hoping that everyone would buy in. In the midst of all of this, my mother, brother, and I had to deal with my dad's alcoholism. A disease that began very early on his life and was maybe inherited from his parents, there was scarcely a day throughout much of my childhood where my father was not stumbling around the trailer park drunk. And every time my dad would drink he would inevitably fly off the handle in fits of rage. The fighting between my parents, the abuse that I experienced personally, the fear that plagued my mind, wore heavily on my young soul. I tried my hardest to pretend to have a normal life and normal family and after a while, I began to believe it. For years, I hid my home life from my friends at school. But by the time I reached the age of twelve, the toxic environment of my home had wounded my soul so deeply, that I found myself ravaged in utter despair.

Every morning when I woke up for school, I would feel a wave of despair rush over my young body. As I would make my way through the day, I would experience frequent spikes of panic and uncontrollable thoughts of suicide. I would often find myself sitting in class with my legs trembling, palms sweating, and mind racing with thoughts of death. As this pattern of depression and anxiety developed, it only drew my soul deeper into despair. I pulled away from friendships and began choosing to be alone rather than face the embarrassment of having a panic attack in front of my friends. As I began drowning under the sea of fear and hopelessness, all of the ambition and dreams for my life began to vanish. I no longer saw a reason for dreaming. My life was clearly going nowhere. I found myself, at the age of twelve, at the very end of my rope.

It is in periods of such utter despair that God tends to work most powerfully. So often, it seems, he will allow us to take the first step off the cliff before he sweeps in to rescue us. The Bible is filled with such examples – Daniel in the lions' den, Shadrach, Meshach, and Abednego in Nebuchadnezzar's fiery furnace, Paul and Silas chained up in prison – the stories of God's last-minute redemptions abound. And just like so many others, it was at this fragile point in my life that God intervened.

Five trailers up from my house lived a very peculiar religious family. That's all the neighbourhood knew about them – that they were strange because they were so very 'religious'. It wasn't that this family went to church that made them odd. It was that they went to church three, sometimes four times a week. The two young girls who lived in the trailer didn't go to school with any of us – they were homeschooled, a fact that made many of us in the neighbourhood very jealous. They wore long dresses, had family dinners, didn't cuss or watch any of the television shows that the rest of us watched. We never really knew what to think of them, but as kids, none of that really seemed important. I began hanging out with them regularly, running around the woods that surrounded our homes, building forts with old wood that we found around the trailer park or exploring the ruins of an old pig farm that lay just on the other side of the stream from our trailer park. We became best friends fast. But every time Wednesday or Sunday rolled around, my friends were not allowed to come outside to play. Instead, the family packed into their car and headed to church. Nothing was more frustrating than not being able to play with my new friends on 'church days'. You know how it goes. We always seem to want something the most on the days we can't have it. (Like Chick-fil-A on Sundays!)

One Saturday when we were playing together, one of my friends proposed a solution to the problem of not being able to hang out on Sundays. She suggested that I come to church with them in the morning. At the time, I remember thinking that this was an ingenious way to subvert her parents' strict rules and get to have some extra time with my best friends. It seemed like a great idea. I ran back to my house and asked my mom if it would be okay if I went to church in the morning and she happily granted me permission. I was thrilled! We were going to get to play with each other on a *Sunday*. At least, that's what I thought the plan was. But my friends, like all good religious people, had another intention in mind.

When we arrived at my friend's church the next morning, I was terrified. As someone who didn't grow up in church, I had no clue what to expect. Was there a secret handshake? Special words? Did I stand out as an 'unbeliever'? I clung tightly to the side of my friends, waiting for the moment when we'd break away from the church service and go play. Instead, my friends' parents led me to a separate classroom for Junior Highers while the girls went off to their high school class. I was stunned. I thought that I'd come to church to have more time to hang out with my friends. Instead, they were sending me to a Sunday school class by myself. I had no clue what people did in Sunday school. I had no clue what the correct behaviour was, and I certainly wasn't prepared to answer any questions about God or the Bible. I was a fish out of water. As I sat in the back of the Sunday school classroom and the charismatic youth leader opened up the Bible and talked about the story of Jonah, I could feel my body trembling. The room was filled with kids my age, with their Bibles open, singing the songs, and answering the questions that the youth pastor shouted out. For the first time in my life, I softly uttered a prayer, 'God, please don't let him call on me. Please God. Please God.' I was terrified. I somehow managed to get through the entire class without being called on, and as soon as the Sunday school bell rang, I dashed out of the classroom, down the hall to the church sanctuary where I knew my friends would be waiting for me.

When I finally found them in the sea of people gathered for worship, I realised that there would be no playing with each other this morning. It had all been a ploy to get me to come to church. My friend's mother pulled us over to the pew and sat us down for the service. I looked out over the sanctuary, seeing the sea of faces singing their songs of worship together, in bright pastel dresses and nicely pressed suits, there was something about this great group of people that both creeped me out and intrigued me. When the pastor opened his Bible, he began preaching a fiery message about the saving power of God. His words echoed through the sanctuary, in a way that reverberated through my young heart. He really seemed to believe what he said. He wasn't like the Catholic priests I had seen at my cousin's baptism. This guy seemed to really be speaking from the depths of his heart. There was just something about this place, these people, something about them that stirred in my heart. I couldn't put a name to what this was, but I knew that I wanted to learn more. As the service ended, I dreaded the thought of getting in the car and going back home to my dysfunctional family. Something about this church felt like home in a way that my home didn't. I had completely forgotten about my dashed dreams of having time to play with my friends on Sunday mornings. Instead, something was aroused within me, almost as if a small flame had been lit, and its warmth only seemed to grow brighter. The next Sunday, I arrived at my neighbour's house early in the morning, dress shirt pressed and clip-on tie secured, ready to go back to church. I was actually excited to go, not to hang out with my friends, but to get a taste of home once again.

I continued attending the church week after week, and also began making friends with some of the kids in the youth group. After attending for about three months, I decided to attend a youth rally that the youth pastor was hosting one evening in the church basement. He promised that it would be a time of 'Food, fun, and fellowship', and that we would be hearing from a very special guest speaker. When my friends and I arrived at church on the Friday evening of the rally, caffeinated and ready for some 'Spirit-filled fun', I wasn't prepared for what I was going to experience. After attending church for a couple of months, I had begun to feel pressure from my new community to make a decision about following Jesus. Talks about my eternal destiny became frequent occurrences and fear of going to Hell if I died began to emerge in my heart. I had liked what I had been hearing about this Jesus guy, and felt that if he could really do what my pastor said he could do, then I should give it a try. But I just wasn't sure how.

After a couple of hours of playing dodgeball, eating baby food, and duct-taping each other to the wall (if you grew up in youth group, you'll understand that these are fairly typical things that are done for 'fun'), we all returned to the church basement to hear a message from our guest speaker. My youth pastor announced that the speaker for tonight was a former Major League Baseball Player from the Baltimore Orioles. My entire youth group gasped in excitement. I, on the other hand, barely knew what baseball was. But I pretended to be excited with everyone else. The speaker approached the stage. He was a tall, burly, African-American man with a rich, deep preacher voice. His name was Reverend Pat Kelly, and he began to recount his life story, telling how he had grown up and lived a life that was far from God, filled with all of the world's pleasures – women, drugs, fame, and fortune. He told about how in the midst of all of this success, he felt profoundly lost and hopeless in life. He told how another baseball player cared enough to sit down and share the Gospel of Jesus Christ with him and how God entered his life and radically redeemed him from himself. He then turned to us and pleaded with us to give our lives over to Christ, promising that if we did, God would take all of our circumstances, good, bad, and everything in between, and redeem them for his glory. He spoke of how deeply God loved us, how the Father was ready to embrace us as his children if we would only come to him.

I can't explain what happened that night, but as Reverend Kelly was making his invitation to our youth group, God's Spirit moved. Almost instantly, about a dozen of us teenagers began weeping. I was one of them, tears streaming down my face uncontrollably. My heart felt as though it literally radiated warmth within my chest and I felt what I can only describe as the Love of God beckoning to me through the words of this preacher. Reverend Kelly asked us to come forward and pray with him if we wanted to surrender our lives to Christ, and immediately, I sprung up from my seat and made my way to Reverend Kelly. I looked around, and nearly a dozen other young people were standing alongside me. We gathered together and prayed the 'Sinners' Prayer', inviting Jesus to come into our hearts, forgive us of our sins, and use us for his purposes. As I prayed each word out loud through my tears, I felt as if God was actually cleansing my heart and embracing me in his arms. When the prayer was over, I took a deep breath, looked up, and smiled. I felt like a new person.

After the rally that night, I ran home from my neighbour's house and burst through the door. My mom was sitting in our living room and was caught off guard by my urgent entry. I turned to her and said, 'Mom, I got redeemed tonight!' She looked at me quizzically, and said, 'That's great, Sweetie!' I smiled at her and ran to my room where I pulled out a notebook and recorded my 'Testimony', the word I had heard other church people use to talk about the story of their salvation experience. I stayed up well past my bedtime that night, reading the Bible and praying, feeling a true sense of connection to God and a newness of life, even at twelve years old. In the days and weeks following, I became a zealous evangelist and devoted studier of the Bible. I would wake up early every morning to pray, read the Bible, and watch Dr Charles Stanley, a famous televangelist, preach a message before I went to school. I began wearing a large wooden cross around my neck each day and handed out pamphlets explaining the Gospel to every one of my friends. Every week, I made sure that I went to church as often as I could, which often meant 4-6 times in one week. My parents, friends, and teachers looked on with scepticism and amusement, wondering if this new religious phase would ever wear off. But as time went on and my zeal for Jesus only increased, it became clear that my life had been transformed. I knew it, and everyone around me knew it too.

As time went on, though, the honeymoon phase began to wear off. Though my zeal and passion for God only continued to increase, I came face to face with the first major hurdle to my faith. God had saved me, of that I was sure. I believe that he loved me and had a plan for my life. But I was caught off guard when my life's circumstances didn't begin to change. In fact, they seemed to get worse. I still dealt with the same fear and anxieties of living with an alcoholic father as I had before coming to Christ. My parents still fought often. We still struggled financially. I still suffered from panic attacks and spent many nights on my knees, begging God to remove me from these circumstances. I couldn't understand how he could be a loving Father who would allow me to continue to face such hardships and abuse. Even after my life-transforming encounter with Jesus, I was left to wonder 'Why?' Why did God place me in such a dysfunctional family? Why would God allow me to suffer so much pain? Why did God wait so long to intervene in my life? Why, why, why?

One night during an argument with my dad, I ran into my room and opened my Bible. This was the only thing I knew to do in the midst of distress. My Bible fell open to the book of Job. It's a strange book, sitting all alone in the middle of the Bible. I hadn't heard my pastor preach about it, and I rarely heard it quoted. This lack of interaction piqued my curiosity and I began reading through this strange book, asking God to speak to me through it. The story was confusing to me as a new Christian and many questions arose. For instance, why was Satan in heaven having a conversation with God? Is that really how that works? And why would God allow Satan to hurt Job, his faithful servant? It didn't seem to make much sense. As I continued reading, I began to feel empathetic towards Job's suffering. Though Job and I went through *very* different trials, our circumstances both seemed equally perplexing. If anyone seemed to get that pain and confusion that I was going through, it was Job. As I read, I came to chapter 23, as Job was responding to the complaints of his not-so-wise friend Eliphaz. Job says:

'(1-2) Even today my problems are more than I can handle.
In spite of my groans, God's hand is heavy on me.
I wish I knew where I could find him!
I wish I could go to the place where he lives!
I would state my case to him. (10) But he knows every step I take.
When he has put me to the test,
I'll come out as pure as gold.'

Job's words pierced through my heart. Even though I had come to know God and believed that he loved me, I wondered why he had continued to allow me to go through so much pain. I sensed that Job was going through a similar sense of confusion. Job, too, was left on his knees before God asking 'Why?' He felt that his problems were *'more than he could handle'* and he begged

God to remove them from him. I felt like I had a faithful friend walking alongside me in my suffering. But what really stuck out were the words that Job spoke at the end of verse 10. *'When he has put me to the test, I'll come out as pure as gold'.* I read in the commentary notes at the bottom of the page in my Bible that Job was referencing the image of a refining fire. The commentator explained that the image that was being alluded to was that of a hot fire being used to remove impurities from tarnished gold, in order to make it shine brighter than before. What Job was saying, then, was that the trials that he faced were actually being used to make him stronger, to help him shine brighter. He didn't gloss over his immense pain – the entire book is filled with cries, pleas, and prayers to God, agonising over the losses and afflictions he faced. But even in the midst of all of this, Job still believed that God could redeem his circumstances. Even though it seemed that God was not listening to his pleas for deliverance, Job still believed that God was good and would ultimately transform his pain into blessing.

Could God be using my dysfunctional circumstances to refine me? I wondered. Could God have a plan for all of this pain and suffering that I was going through? Could there be a redemptive purpose to it all? My spirit began to lift. I sensed God was telling me that he had not abandoned me in my hour of need. That, though he did not orchestrate the suffering I was facing, he would still work to redeem it. To take the broken pieces of my life and fashion from them something brand new. This shift in perspective changed the way that I looked at my circumstances. I began to shift from blaming God for my suffering to seeking God in the midst of my pain, asking him to redeem it. And nearly a decade later, God has indeed begun the messy and beautiful process of redeeming it all.

In life we will all face suffering of many different kinds. Of that we can be certain. But whatever the circumstance we find ourselves in may be, I have come to believe that all of it can be redeemed. Many of us will face abuse and injustice that is so dark it cannot be written in words. But even that kind of pain doesn't have to destroy us. We can chose to live our lives with open wounds, allowing ourselves to be ever enslaved to our circumstances, or we can submit our suffering to God, and trust that somehow, in some way, he will take the pieces of our broken lives and create something beautiful beyond description. It may not be easy to see in the midst of the trial, but if we grab hold of the hope of redemption, we can find a renewed sense of resolve that will help us to endure even the darkest of trials.

It is this hope that has become the fuel for my journey. It is this lesson that has enabled me to keep walking, pressing on, following the wild winds of the Spirit of God.

4

Other

*Any person who, with all the sincerity of heart,
is in search for God, on land or in the sea,
is worthy of respect.*

Riaz Ahmed Gohar Shahi

You know the old cliché – 'You can't judge a book by its cover.'
Well, it's not true. I always judge books by their covers and rarely
have I ever been wrong. If the cover is cluttered, too flashy, or
too bland, than the chances are that the writing is cluttered,
flashy, or bland as well. But there have those rare times when I
have been wrong and a book that had a terrible cover, that I was
totally uninterested in, ended up changing my life. I struggle with
judging not only books, but entire groups of people based on *their*
covers too. I can't tell you how many times I have heard that *those
people* are heretics or *that person* is unbiblical and then judged
not only the person (or people) that I initially heard about, but all
those that are even remotely connected to them.

I'll give you an example – when I was still a Baptist, I believed
that any church that used the NIV Bible were sell-outs and
heretics. Seriously. Our church was a 'KJV-Only' church, which
literally meant the only English translation of the Bible that we
considered to be inspired by God was the King James Version

translated at the command of the King of England in the 1600s. Strangely enough, I can recall my youth pastor saying to me that 'The KJV was good enough for the Apostle Paul so it's good enough for me!' Don't ask me how they made that work. The point is that I was taught to believe that if any church or Christian used any other version of the Bible, then they didn't have the word of God. This left a *very* small group of people who actually were preaching the word of God in our perspective. Most so-called Evangelical and *even* Baptist churches had switched over to the heretical NIV translation. They said it was because it was 'easier to understand', but we knew the real reason people loved it so much – it diluted the truth!

So as a young, 12 year old Christian boy, I was devoted to the King James Bible. Or at least I said I was. After trying desperately to fall in love with the King James Version of the Bible, alas, my young mind just didn't easily understand the old English of the Bible. So, every night before bed, when I had set aside time to do my devotions (Evangelical lingo for 'read the Bible and pray'), I would secretly read a New International Version Children's Bible that I hid underneath my bed like a dirty magazine. I felt so incredibly guilty for using it, but it just seemed to make *so much* more sense. When I would pray, I would ask God to forgive me for my unfaithfulness to his *true* word (the KJV) and to still take the bits of truth that remained in the NIV to feed my soul. And God did just that. I learned more and grew more through the NIV than I ever did with the KJV. But I couldn't let anyone know that. Because the only people who used the NIV were heretics.

After being forced to leave my Baptist church because of a number of complicated situations, I ended up attending an Evangelical megachurch close to my trailer park. As I walked into the auditorium on my first Sunday visiting, I was filled with conflicting thoughts. I was in awe at how cool this church felt – the comfy theatre seat, the big stage with lights, the band that sounded just like the ones I heard on the radio. But I also believed that these people were heretics. This kind of church *couldn't* be a gospel preaching one. It was too big. They had drums. And *they used the NIV.* I know this whole Bible translation thing might seem a bit excessive to many readers, but I cannot express to you just how serious an issue I had been taught this was. As I sat through the service, I judged everything that was happening. I tried desperately to fit everything I saw and heard into the box marked 'heretical.' Every song sung, every trippy lighting effect, every word the pastor preached. But the problem was that the more I listened, the more I experienced, the more I encountered the people around me genuinely worshipping God and receiving his word, the harder it became for me call these people heretics. Every week as I returned to this community I began meeting more and more people and falling more in love with their passion for Jesus and being a community centred on grace. It didn't take long for me to decide that what I had been taught about those who weren't KJV-Only fundamentalists was wrong. These people simply *weren't* heretics. Their love for Jesus and commitment to his word poured forth in a way that I had never experienced. These people were my brothers and sisters. As soon as I began to put down my walls of judgement and fear of 'the other', I began to be fundamentally transformed by God's work in and through this community.

Fear and demonisation of 'the other' is one of the biggest problems with Christianity (and perhaps *every* religion) today. Anthropologists have long understood that one of the fundamental methods that human use to create a unified community to unite *against* a common enemy. Nothing can bind a group of people more tightly together than coming together with a common disdain and even hatred for a person or a group of people. History is filled with many unfortunate examples of how coming together against a common enemy has brought great unity among some of the most divided groups. Whether it was Adolf Hitler and Nazi Germany coming together against the Jewish people, the great unity that enabled the Nazis to create such a massive movement came from convincing Germany that the Jewish people were the problem, the great enemy of their flourishing. The problem was that they Jewish people *were not* the enemies of the German people. There was no secret plot among the Jewish people to undermine 'the Aryan race.' What Hitler and the Nazi party were saying about the Jewish people had no basis in reality. But because a large number of Germans had been convinced by the Nazi propaganda, they weren't interested in finding out the truth. They had no reason to *ask* a Jewish person if Hitler's accusations were true. The Jewish people became the 'other' to Nazi Germany and had to be expelled at all costs. And all of it was based on misinformation. Lies. But never before had Germany been so united. The reason so many people submitted to the horrendous leadership of Hitler was because he actually *seemed* to be helping the nation. Germany was united and strong like it had never been before. That unity came from gathering together against a common enemy – the Jewish people.

While the example of the Holocaust is an extreme example, I use it because I think it accurately shows the potential for what can occur when a group of people engages in the process of demonising and marginalising their 'others.' The camaraderie that forms as a group labels another group or person 'heretics' or 'false teachers' binds people together in a way few other things can. It makes sense, then, that in Evangelicalism, those who are in positions of leadership often engage in 'heresy hunting', looking for those both within their ranks and outside of their circles who claim to be Christians but do not *seem* to agree with their theology or the way they do ministry. If someone is identified as a potential threat, usually based on a sound bite or rumour, they can send out one tweet, write one blog post, or preach one sermon and mobilise an army of people to unite against this 'other.' Usually, as this process occurs, the 'other' is never actually confronted personally. No one asks them to clarify. No one seeks to understand his or her perspective. Because that's really not the purpose of the marginalisation. While I am convinced that those who engage in the 'heresy hunting' do not often have bad motives and actually believe that what they are doing is right, helpful, and good for their community. I believe that the real (often subconscious) purpose is to maintain unity within the group. That's why this very twisted process continues to occur over and over again among and within most religious communities.

But, as with most every wayward tendency of humans, there is a better way. There is another means to fostering unity within our communities that brings life and breeds openness. There is a way that disarms both the 'us' and the 'them' and creates, in the midst of our great diversity and complexity, a 'we'. And that way is *love*. Love is what has the power to bring divided groups together. Love has the power to dispel the fear that arises when we first witness someone doing something *other* than what we have always done. Love has the power to bring peace, understanding, and humanity back to the 'other' that we feel compelled to objectify and marginalised. As the Apostle Paul describes in the book of Ephesians, it was Love Incarnate that was willing to sacrifice his right to be right, the knowledge that his way was *indeed* the better way, and give himself fully and freely on the cross for those who despised and marginalised him. And through his act of self-giving, he destroyed the barriers that divide all people – barriers of race, religion, culture, creed, colour, class, sexuality, and every other aspect that we have used to segregate throughout time. At the cross, Jesus revealed to us the way to deal with our fear and our impulse to scapegoat those who look, think, act, or worship differently – release it. Instead of allowing our fear of the other to keep us from interacting with each other, Jesus shows us that we must be willing to go and be *with* and *among* those who are different. We must embrace, befriend, and sacrificially give ourselves to those whom we're supposed to fear. In doing so, we will often discover that our 'other' is not so different after all. That no matter what our differences might be, our 'other' is more often than not genuinely seeking for truth, for life, for love. And even *if* we discover that their motives are not pure, it is our self-giving and sacrifice, not our demonisation and blog battles, that will win them over to the truth.

A mentor of mine once told me an African proverb that summed up this principle beautifully:

'When I saw him from afar, I thought he was a monster.
When he got closer, I thought he was an animal.
When he got closer, I recognised that he was a human.
When we were face to face, I realised that he was my brother.'

How easy it is for us to demonise from a distance. But when we stand face to face with our supposed enemy, it is hard to hate. Because when we begin to talk *to* each other instead of *about* each other, we are able to see, to hear, and to sense the heart of those with whom we differ. We begin to understand their true motives and intentions. We begin to sense the heart behind their thoughts and sound bites. If only we would be willing to take the time to understand one another instead of accepting and propagating hearsay and slander, then maybe we could see more unity within the Church. If we ceased our accusations (which, according the Scriptures, is an action that Satan engages in, not God – Rev. 12:10) and instead sought to follow the way of Jesus, the God who is *with* us, we might begin to bring into reality what Jesus prayed for his Church just hours before his death – that they may be *one*.

But even beyond ecclesial unity, the message and methods of Jesus should compel us to seek to love and understand even those with whom we fundamentally disagree – those of different faiths, different sexualities, and different political ideologies. Jesus never called his people to be engaged in slandering, attacking, or even arguing and defending ourselves to those who differ from us. Instead, he calls us to be *with* them. To love them. To befriend them. Not with hidden motives to convert them to our way of thinking and believing, but with genuine desire to understand who they are. That is, after all, what Jesus did throughout most of his public ministry. From what we can tell, Jesus spent more time eating, drinking, and lounging with 'tax collectors and sinners' than explaining the Roman Roadmap to Heaven or undermining their belief system. The Jesus-way of evangelism is to *love*. Love means accepting with much patience and humility the differences in the 'other.' Love means being honest and authentic about what we believe and think, but to do so in a way that isn't intended to offend but rather to inspire awe in the 'other.' This is a lesson I wish I had learned much earlier on in my journey of faith.

During my high-school years, I was very involved in inter-faith dialogue. What that really means is that I liked to argue with anyone who wasn't a fundamentalist Christian like me. Throughout my four years, I spent countless hours debating with Mormons, Muslims, Wiccans, Pagans, Atheists, Non-Religious and of course, the Methodists, trying to convert them from their way of false teaching to my way, or rather, *the way*. Because of my 'boldness' to stand up for my faith, I even got the nicknames 'Bible-Boy' and 'Ishmahel' (don't ask) among my peers and even got nominated 'Most likely to "save" the world' in my senior year. (Pun intended.)

During my senior year I became friends with two Muslims, Siama and Ahmed, who were in my Home Economics class. For the entire course of the year, I would strike up debates among them as I tried to convince them that their God was a false god and convert them to Christianity. The problem was I didn't really know much about Islam other than that it was false. Most of the information I had gathered had come from the apologetics training I received at my church and from John Hagee's sermons on TBN – both sources who probably had never actually spoken to a Muslim apart from in attempting to convert them. I 'knew' that Muslims worshipped a Pagan moon-god named Allah, that they were commanded to kill anyone who didn't believe their false gospel, that they were out to destroy America, and that they also worshipped cows. With this information as my foundation for evangelism, you can imagine how offended (and frankly amused) my Muslim friends were when I began to refute these supposed beliefs of theirs. What I quickly began to realise is that nearly *all* of the information I had learned from my church about Islam was simply false. My friends took time to refute each outlandish claim from the Quran itself, proving to me that Allah was *not* a moon god but the *same* God of Jews and Christians, that they were commanded to love those of different religions, not kill them, that they had no desire to 'take over America' and that the worship of cows was not a Muslim ritual, but a Hindu one.

They too, however, proved to be relatively uninformed about Christianity and all of its complexity, often mixing Catholic and Protestant beliefs, and throwing in strange and off the wall ideas that I am quite sure no Christian has ever believed. So eventually, our mutual ignorance of each other's faith cancelled each other out and we found ourselves at a stalemate, a common ground beyond our misunderstandings, where we could begin a healthy and open dialogue about the similarities and differences between Christianity and Islam. Now, we were all still young and zealous, so I would continue to try to convince them to recant their beliefs and become Christians and they continued to try to get me to convert to Islam, but our face to face dialogues helped us begin to comprehend with some degree of clarity what the other group *actually* believed. And as we did, we began to discover the immense amount of common ground we shared – believing Jesus was the Messiah, longing for his second coming, the importance of prayer, the inspiration of the Bible, and many other shocking areas where our belief systems seemed to parallel. None of us were successful in our attempt to convert the other, but we did walk away with more respect, more understanding, and more humility towards each other. From that period on, my posture towards Islam has been fundamentally different because when I spoke about Muslims, I was no longer speaking about some vague group over there, but was talking about my friends Siama and Ahmed. Real people who I loved and appreciated, and who defied all of the stereotypes and misnomers that were spread about their faith. And even though I still have a number of disagreements with Muslim theology I now have respect for their belief system that I never could have gained if I hadn't had the opportunity to sit down and get to know Siama and Ahmed.

The point of loving 'the other' is not to become relativists. When I am speaking about loving our 'others', I am not saying that we must agree with everything (or even anything) that they believe or stand for. We may find in our face to face dialogue that much of what we thought about them was correct or even that we don't really *like* the person or people. And that's okay. Jesus doesn't call us to like everybody – there are *some* people that I will *never like*. But it's those very people that I often need to work the hardest to get to know and to understand. For when I am actually sitting across the table with someone, even if I discover that I don't particularly like or agree with them, I still can see that they are human beings, just like me. They are not an idea. They are not a concept. They are a real, living and breathing human being who is just trying to figure everything out, just like I am. In my experience, I have often found myself wanting to bang my head into a wall after having some difficult conversations with people with whom I disagree. 'Why don't they get it?!' I often asked. But part of loving is sacrificing our ego's need to be right. Part of loving is realising that all of us are on the same journey, seeking the same things, but find ourselves at different places. When we are able to acknowledge and accept this reality; we are freed from the desire to force others into our systems, our beliefs, and our points of view. Instead, we are able to value every person for *who* they are and appreciate the journey on which they find themselves. We don't need anyone to conform to our perspective because we have humbled ourselves to realise that we too are on a journey and all of our knowledge, *especially theological knowledge,* is just our best attempt to describe the Reality that we experience and interact with at this stage of our life.

As followers of Jesus, we must recommit ourselves to Jesus' way of life. We must be willing to be *with* those whom we see as our theological, political, ideological, cultural, racial, and sexual 'others'. Until we are willing to take up the cross of self-sacrifice and follow in the footsteps of our Rabbi, we will continue to perpetuate the often violent cycle of 'othering'. We will continue to misrepresent, misunderstand, and marginalise men and women who are created in the image of God and pulsating with life and creativity, in order to create a faulty coherency within our own community. We will continue to participate in life, not as those who incarnate the Love of God, but as those who participate in propagating falsehoods and misunderstanding about our brothers and sisters. We will continue to miss out on the beauty and diversity of what God is doing just beyond the walls of our community. We will continue to fail to be a witness to the God who took on flesh to be *with* us, positioning ourselves against him as his enemies. But when we are willing to walk in the way of Love, to embody the light of Christ to everyone we encounter, we open ourselves to see and understand the journeys of so many other people. When we place ourselves in humility before those who are different from us, we not only honour the perspective and experience of our brother or sister, but we have the opportunity to learn and have our eyes opened to a new way of being. Because our big, wild, and diverse God is at work in millions of systems, philosophies, cultures, religions, and people beyond our own. The more we are willing to let God teach us through those who are different, the more our own spiritual lives are enriched and the more we become the reconcilers that we are called to be.

5

War

Young Christians are ready for peace.
We are ready to lay down our arms.
We are ready to stop waging war and start washing feet.

Rachel Held Evans

'*I may never march in the infantry, ride in the cavalry, shoot the artillery. I may never fly o'er the enemy, But I'm in the Lord's army! Yes Sir!*'

This song was one of my first exposures to the Christian faith. I remember singing it proudly, with my hand over my heart and head held high in my Baptist pre-school. I wasn't sure what most of those words meant, but I remember thinking that it was really cool that I was in *God's* army. I didn't remember ever formally enlisting, but hey, my teachers told me I was in, and I was more than happy to be a soldier. What other five-year-old could say that?

From the earliest days of my life, I've understood the Christian faith in militaristic terms. When I became a follower of Jesus at the age of twelve, I drew heavily on these early memories of Christianity, and began to frame my new life in Christ as enlisting in a spiritual militia of sorts. My pastor spoke of spiritual warfare against the forces of darkness that were prevailing in our culture. The Christian televangelists I watched incessantly talked about how Christians were being persecuted and how we would need to pick up our swords (which supposedly meant Bibles) and go to war against the forces that sought to destroy Christ's Kingdom.

I began to understand that the militaristic language I had learned in preschool wasn't just cute imagery that they put in kids' songs. It was serious. I was really supposed to believe that I was in a literal battle against the forces of darkness. This new reality that I lived in was always abuzz with talk of the latest 'threats' to the body of Christ, calls to go to battle against the ever-growing list of enemies of the Kingdom, and talk of 'taking back ground' that had been stolen by 'the devil' which usually meant 'liberal politicians'.

I understood that for the time being, my duty as a Christian in the battle was to stand boldly against the enemies of truth that surrounded me in my everyday life. For me, this looked like burning my blink-182 CDs and wearing pro-life buttons on my backpack. But I was also taught to believe that one day, when Jesus returned, I'd actually get the chance to engage in real, flesh and blood warfare. On that day, I'd be given a horse and a sword and we would all ride into Jerusalem poised to destroy, once and for all, the Anti-Christ and all who sided with him (which was everyone who was not a Christian). These thoughts always made me pretty uncomfortable, but at the same time, I believed that this final, bloody battle needed to take place for peace to be established on earth as it is in heaven.

This mindset of warfare continues to be predominant in conservative Christianity. This eschatology (or theology of the end times) is taught to thousands in megachurches and millions by televangelists every single week. And even though the average Christian isn't *actually* militaristic, this mindset of war does affect the way we interact with the people and culture that surround us. We begin to see everything in our world as increasingly dark and hostile to us and our faith. We begin to view every news story through the lens of our eschatology, believing that every political decision that doesn't align with our worldview and every artefact of pop culture that doesn't expressly promote our values as a sign of the end times and as an attack on our faith.

It's this impulse to defend our faith against perceived threats that has made Christians more known for what we're against than what we're for. The now infamous Barna poll that was conducted back in 2007 revealed that just 3 per cent of all young people from the ages of 16-29 had a favourable view of Evangelical Christianity and 91 per cent said that the most common perception of Christianity was 'anti-homosexual', followed by 87 per cent who said Christians were 'judgemental'. When this poll came out back in 2007 in conjunction with Dave Kinnaman's book *UnChristian*, the Evangelical world was reeling. Churches and denominations came together to seek to find ways to change the culture's perception of the Christian faith. But nearly a decade later, I think it's safe to say that the perception hasn't changed at all, in large part, because it seems that the primary impulse of modern day Christianity is the impulse to defend and go to battle against our culture. When the culture strikes back at the Church, say, by trying to pass legislation that would take away churches' tax-exempt status, we cry persecution, which only further ingrains the war mindset into the consciousness of Christians.

In the early days of my faith, this mindset tinted the way I saw everything in the world. As a boy who already had an anxiety disorder, living my life on the defense was not helpful. Yet, I felt that I had no other choice. If I wasn't defending God's honour, then I was allowing the devil to win. If I wasn't preaching the truth to those who were walking in ways that were dishonouring to God, then I was sending souls to Hell. But when I did confront people in my High School about their ungodly choices – which meant anything from being a different denomination that I believed had 'sold out', to aligning politically with an issue that I believed was at odds with the word of God – I was seen as bigoted, intolerant, and uneducated. Of course, this was to be expected. 'The world hated Jesus', I was told. 'They're going to hate you as well. Just keep standing for the truth.' The burden was unbearable. The work was never done. There was never an opportunity for rest. And that 'peace of God that passes all understanding' that was so often promised to me? It was unattainable. I could never figure out how anybody could possibly be at peace when the attacks against God's kingdom never ceased.

During my freshman year in college, I spent a semester reading through the four Gospels. This was a surprisingly rare exercise for me because I often found Jesus' words incredibly confusing. I was a fan of the Apostle Paul. His words were clear, straightforward, and deeply theological. When Paul wanted to say something, he said it. Jesus, on the other hand, spoke in parables. His words were often cryptic. And most perplexingly, he seemed to have really bad theology. Paul made it clear that salvation was 'by faith alone, through grace'. But Jesus seemed to suggest that we would be ultimately judged based on what we did, how we lived, and not on what we believed. Paul also seemed to speak a lot about false teachers and being at war with the world. Jesus, not so much.

As I read through the words of Jesus over and over again in the Gospel accounts, an overwhelming theme began to emerge. I began to notice that every word of judgement or opposition that Jesus spoke was against *the religious people* and not against the rest of the culture that seemed to be engaging in immoral and ungodly activities. Jesus seemed to be more angered by religious people condemning the rest of the world than with those who were engaged in what was clearly unbiblical behaviour. This isn't to say that Jesus condoned the sin that he encountered – to the contrary. Time and time again, he clearly called sinners to repentance. But as I read the Gospels, I found that I identified more, not with Jesus, but with the scribes and Pharisees, who walked around, always looking for the next person who wasn't doing it right. They walked around convinced that they were in God's favour and had found the way of truth. But Jesus said just the opposite. Instead of lauding the Pharisees for their spiritual superiority, Jesus proclaims that they are 'sons of hell' and 'blind'. Could the same be said of me? In my constant judgement of others for not living up to 'biblical standards', which Jesus seemed to say almost nothing about, was I blind? Was I leading people astray? Was I shutting the door of the Kingdom of Heaven on those who would otherwise have come in?

These questions plagued my soul for a number of months and all the while the answer that I dreaded was astoundingly clear. How could I, one who was so lost and broken when I was found by God, turn around and judge those who were no less broken than I was? How could I believe that God wanted me to wage a holy war against the lost and broken world, when Jesus so clearly demonstrated the opposite? How could I preach a message of condemnation to those with whom I disagreed, when Jesus preached a message of unconditional love, acceptance, and sacrifice for the lost? Could it be that there is another way to live the Christian life? Could it be that the way to transform the world is not through warring against those who live and believe differently, but rather through loving those who are different by welcoming them, just as they are, not seeking to change their minds but rather seeking to introduce them to the Saviour who said that he has come to seek and save the lost?

As I studied the words of Jesus, I actually began to discover for the first time what seemed like genuinely good news. I began to understand that Jesus was indeed the friend of sinners, the God who came to be with us, to love us, and to call us from our misguided way of life to the abundant life that he created us to experience. I began to realise that Jesus didn't see himself as someone who was at war with the world but rather one who came to restore the world. Instead of condemning all of those who walked in ways that were contrary to his own, Jesus instead demonstrated a better way in their presence, which always seemed to result in groups of people turning and following after him. The greatest demonstration of all was, of course, the cross. It was at the cross that my transformation occurred.

Looking through the eyes of the Gospel writers up on that rugged wooden cross, I saw Rabbi Jesus, damned by the religious officials of his day, beaten, and hanging naked before the crowds. I saw him looking down with compassion on all of those who had harmed him and to the common criminals that hung either side of him. I heard him pronouncing forgiveness, grace, and peace on his enemies. It was in this moment I understood for the first time what Jesus meant when he called his disciples to take up their crosses daily and follow him. I understood that to be a follower of Jesus, I was not supposed to be warring against and separating from the world around me, but rather living as a light within the culture, extending to everyone the grace that I myself so desperately needed. I finally understood that God was truly interested in transforming our world not through conquest and battle but through sacrifice and love. My world was being utterly transfigured by this powerful revelation.

This epiphany caused me to feel both convicted and yet deeply comforted. On the one hand, I realised that I had been a religious hypocrite, of the same ilk as the ones who called for Jesus' death because of his unconditional love and acceptance for the non-kosher people with whom he surrounded himself. I had spent so much of my time 'evangelising', telling others why they were wrong instead of showing them the love that Jesus had for them. I had condemned my fellow Christians because they hung out at parties and clubs, while I was spending my Friday night volunteering at my church. I was a Pharisee. I had caused more harm than good to so many people whom God loved so much. I was ashamed. But in the midst of this painful realisation, I was also comforted. Comforted that even as Jesus looked deeply into the eyes of the hypocritical religious men who surrounded him at Golgotha, he was able to extend grace and forgiveness to them. And at the same time, he extended it to me. *To all of us.* Yes, I had caused a lot of damage. Yes, I had fundamentally misrepresented to the world what it looked like to be a follower of Christ. But I had done nothing that God was not willing and able to redeem and restore.

The way of the Gospel is not one of separation, condemnation, or marginalisation. Instead, through the Gospel we are called to be ministers of *reconciliation*. Jesus demonstrated this powerfully on his cross when, in the words of the Apostle Paul, he 'made peace through his blood.' On the cross, Jesus ended the division between the Jew and Gentile, holy and unholy, clean and unclean, chosen and reprobate. On the cross Jesus put an end to all judgement, condemnation, and war. He revealed that the Kingdom of God would not be established through Christianising our culture but by sacrificing our rights, privileges, and positions of power out of love for our neighbours. For our *enemies*. This is indeed 'foolishness' to the world, but it is the wisdom of God.

We have too often forgotten this powerful principle. But one glance at up at the cross is enough to remind us that the way we are to 'win' this world over to the Jesus way is through love, not through legislation. Through listening, not by shouting through megaphones. The way we're going to establish the Kingdom of God is through seeking to build bridges of understanding between those with whom we disagree, not through forcefully attempting to convert them to the 'biblical' way of living. When we attempt to win our culture through forcing them to adhere to our Christian values, we are placing a stumbling block in front of them. We are asking them to attain a standard of 'righteousness' in order to be pleasing to God. What could be more antithetical to the Gospel than that?

During the summer of my freshman year in college, I went on a choir tour to Greece and Cyprus. One of the memories that is seared deep onto my mind was during our tour of Athens. After climbing up the long, rugged staircase that leads to the Acropolis that stands mightily above the city of Athens, we stopped and looked out over the ancient city. The view was breathtaking. As we began to wander around the ancient temple, our tour guide noted that for a number of centuries the Pagan temple to the goddess Athena had actually been converted to a Christian church. Of course, this piqued the interest of a group of Bible college students.

Our guide went on to explain that during Christian 'evangelistic' efforts, a mighty Christian army came speeding towards Athens with the mission of killing everyone in the city who did not profess faith in Christ. The quick-witted people of Athens immediately devised a plan to save themselves and their metropolis, filled with magnificent temples and shrines to their pagan demigods. When the crusaders approached, the Athenians flocked to the banks of the sea and were 'baptised' Christian. Following this magnificent conversion, they made their way back up to the temple of Athena with the crusaders. Yet instead of calling it a temple of Athena, they claimed it was a sanctuary to Mary, the holy mother of God. As you can imagine, this greatly pleased the Christians who believed that Mary was the protector of them on their mission to Christianise the world by force. So these 'evangelisers' moved on, leaving very little damage or bloodshed in their wake. Of course, after the Christians were long gone, the new converts abruptly reverted to their pagan practices. The cunning minds of the Athenians had out-smarted the Christians and saved their lives, their culture, and their religion.

How much of our culture in the West is just like this? How many politicians and celebrities feel compelled to embrace the label 'Christian' in order to appease the powerful Evangelical population? Over the short history of the United States, Christians have continued the legacy of the crusaders, believing we have a divine mandate to 'win our nation for Christ', which, ironically doesn't mean living as lights in our communities, loving our neighbours, doing justice, or even sharing the Gospel. Instead, that means winning positions of cultural and political power and authority and imposing our worldview and values on a nation in which our perspective is increasingly becoming minority. We feel compelled to fight for prayer in our public schools and for Creationism to be taught in the classroom, but what part of the great commission does that fit into? We vocally war against legislation to support same-sex couples' civil right to be married under the law, claiming that marriage is 'our' institution. But when did Jesus, or Paul, or Peter, or *anyone* ever ask us to do that? As we force our worldview and values on a nation that cannot relate to them, is it any wonder that there are such negative perceptions of Christianity?

Because if *that's* Christianity even *I* want **nothing** to do with it. Thankfully, that's not the faith modeled by Jesus. That's not the way of the Kingdom. The truth is that the Good News of the Gospel is *not* actually synonymous with Fox News ... or MSNBC for that matter. It's better than that. It transcends political, social, ethnic, sexual, religious, economic, and gender divisions and brings us all together as *one new humanity* in Christ. The whole concept of warring against our culture or against non-Christians is an idea that is completely foreign to the Scriptures because the Christian way isn't one of shoving our ideas and values down the throats of our neighbours, but is instead, finding creative ways to live as followers of Christ within every culture. If the example of the early church tells us anything, it is that the way of Jesus can and must be adapted to and moulded to fit within different cultural contexts. Christians are called to be creative, discovering innovative ways of expressing our faith in ways that are consistent with our cultural context.

For example, in Acts 17, the Apostle Paul is preaching to crowds of Greek scholars and philosophers. When he describes the Gospel to these well-educated, cosmopolitan men, he references an eclectic mix of Greek poetry, religious tradition, and philosophy to communicate what it is that Christianity is all about. In the centuries following, as Christianity spread throughout the world, missionaries adapted the message and practices of the Christian faith to reflect the predominant cultural norms in each society. In many pagan cultures, the Sun god became the 'Son of God', using the same images and icons that the pagans had been familiar with but adapting the narrative of the Sun god to reflect the Gospel account of Jesus. This wasn't a way of watering down the message of the faith nor was it a sly tactic in order to trick converts. Rather, it was understood that because of the universality of the Gospel message, it could and should be incarnated into each culture, representing God's unique word of salvation to every nation, tribe, tongue, and group of people.

The modern pursuit of winning over the culture is ultimately a pursuit of power and domination. In the Western World, Christians have enjoyed a position of privilege for centuries. We have been at the forefront of the creation of culture and have often been the ones who have held the highest positions of power in the world. And while many great contributions have been made by Christianity because of its position of influence over the centuries, the truth seems to be that whenever Christianity is given power and prominence, it ceases to be authentic Christianity. Whenever Christians become obsessed with the pursuit of political power they fundamentally fall out of step with the way of Jesus. Jesus demonstrated this time and time again in his life. The least are the greatest in the Kingdom of God and the first will be the last. Those with the least privilege and power, according to Jesus, are the ones with the most potential to change the world.

History has even proven this. Major transformation has never come from the White House or Westminster. Instead, those who have changed our world for the better are those who had little power, prestige, or privilege. Mother Teresa, Martin Luther King Jr., Mahatma Gandhi to name a few of the more popular examples. But there are countless others who live their lives according to the subversive rhythms of the Kingdom of God each and every day and who are are bringing substantial transformation to their communities, cultures, and world. We may never know their names. Their communities may marginalise them. They may never have much material wealth in this life. But the truth is that God is pleased to make his appeal and to work through these men and women – the least of these. At the time of the writing of this book, I have been living in Washington D.C. for just a few months. But even after this small amount of time living and engaging in the political sphere, I have already become utterly convinced that if the hope of our nation and world lies in politics and lawmakers, then we are most certainly doomed. Policies and laws have can have substantial effects on the lives of a nation's citizens, but if we are looking for true, substantial transformation, it can only come by way of men and women who live humbly and subversively as incarnations of Christ in their culture.

Not through culture wars. Not through legislation. Only through love.

6

Grey

At some point, life goes from being fairly simple to incredibly complex. I am not sure of the exact moment when it happened for me, but I can clearly remember the days when I believed that every question of life could be solved with a simple answer.

The world was either created by God or it wasn't.
The Bible was either totally true or totally false.
You were either a Christian or you weren't.
You either preached my tribe's version of the Gospel or you were a false teacher.
You were either going to heaven or hell.

When everything is black and white, you can go through life with relative ease. There is a great deal of confidence that comes from believing that you are on the correct side of a two-sided coin.

But all of that can change in an instant. One conversation, one encounter, one moment of epiphany where the world that once seemed so black and white turns to an unidentifiable shade of grey. The beliefs that we once held to be absolute and certain suddenly become subjective and unclear. The answers that we once held to so tightly dissolve and new, terrifying questions emerge. And in a moment, everything in our life is up for scrutiny.

The first time many of us experienced a small glimpse of this shift is that fateful day when we realised Santa Claus wasn't real. Do you remember that experience? For me, it came a few days after Christmas when I was playing in my parents' bedroom. I was crawling around and ended up wiggling my way under their bed. To my surprise, I found a bunch of rolls of wrapping paper; the same *exact* kind that Santa and his elves had used to wrap my Christmas presents just a few days before. I was shocked. How did mom get Santa's wrapping paper? It all seemed quite suspicious. When I confronted my mom about my discovery, she attempted to concoct some excuse. 'Parents actually help Santa and the elves wrap the presents on Christmas Eve', she said. 'Are you kidding me? This magical elf that flies around the world delivering presents to everyone in one night couldn't take care of wrapping the presents?' I thought in my young mind.

Yeah, *right*.

One discovery of wrapping paper under our parents' bed is all that it takes to unravel one of the *most* important myths of our childhood. Similarly, it's the small discoveries that emerge as we grow in life that begin to reveal some deep questions about our faith. One high school biology class is all that it takes to begin asking some serious questions about the book of Genesis and the origins of humanity. One conversation with a close friend who is struggling to be gay and Christian is all that it takes to begin wondering if the interpretation of Leviticus we heard in Sunday School is actually applicable in today's context. One life-shattering tragedy is all that it takes to begin rethinking the whole notion of the 'sovereignty' of God.

When these questions emerge, we usually have one of two responses. Either we begin to doubt the reliability of our faith or we cling more tightly to the cut-and-dried answers that we have been given and try to suppress the validity of the experiences we had that made room for these questions to surface. The latter response is very understandable. For many of us, our faith is the very ground of our existence. We could not imagine what it would be like to live a life without it. When doubts emerge, we fear that if we allow room for even one question, the whole structure by which we live our lives will crumble.

I can clearly remember the night that I had my first true encounter with doubt. It was within the first year of my becoming a Christian. One evening I was lying on my couch watching the History Channel's pre-Easter marathon of shows about Jesus and the Bible. The show I was watching was about the historicity of the resurrection of Christ, which of course, is the very cornerstone of the Christian faith. As I watched the programme, I scoffed at the poor arguments that were being waged by the secular historians about the scientific likelihood that something like the resurrection could have occurred. What did these people know, anyways? It was just when I thought that this show had absolutely failed its attempt to disprove the resurrection that a biblical scholar appeared on the screen and read a quote from the Gospel of Matthew – '*His disciples came by night and stole him away while we were asleep*' (Matthew 28:13). The scholar made the case that one of the theories used to disprove the resurrection of Jesus was that his disciples had stolen his body and claimed he had risen, and he used this text to support his claim. When I heard this, I immediately ran and grabbed my Bible to check if it was actually written there. To my horror, it was. There, in black and white, clear as day, was biblical proof that Jesus' disciples had staged the resurrection. How could this be possible? How could the Church have missed this for so long?

Now, I know what you're thinking. The Gospel doesn't *actually* say that this is what happened. That verse is part of a larger story about how the Roman Guards were paid to make up this lie to tell the government officials in order to dispute the disciples' claim that Jesus' had risen. But in this moment, I didn't think to look at the context. I was thirteen years old for goodness' sake. All that

I knew was that Matthew 28:13 said that the disciples came and stole Jesus body at night. And the discovery of this verse literally paralysed me. I began to sweat. I felt a knot form in the middle of my stomach. An intense wave of depression seized me like I had never experienced before. The message that had saved my life had been exposed as false. Jesus hadn't risen from the dead, after all. It was all a lie.

That night was literally the darkest night of my life. The next morning, I stayed in my bed and refused to get up to go to school. The life had been drained out of me. My faith had been destroyed. How could I possibly go on?

Later that afternoon, I found enough strength to call my youth minister to explain to him my dreadful discovery. I was prepared for him to drop the phone in shock as I told him about what the Bible actually taught about the resurrection of Jesus. But as soon as the words came out of my mouth, I heard laughter on the other end of the line. I was absolutely dumbfounded. What could possibly be so funny? How could he possibly find this situation laughable? My youth pastor asked me to open up my Bible and we read through the entire chapter in the Gospel together. And in an instant, I had realised my mistake. And I began to sob uncontrollably. I was so relieved to discover that according to the Bible, Jesus had, in fact, risen from the dead, and the explanation given by the Roman guards was a lie. I felt like I had been saved all over again.

I tell that story to illustrate the effects that doubts can have on a believer. If we embrace them, they can lead us into very dark places. And what happens when the doubts don't have simple explanations like mine? What if the pat answers our pastor throws out to us just don't do the trick? What if, at the end of the day, our questions never find a satisfactory answer?

Some of my first real doubts were simultaneously terrifying and exhilarating. When I was a senior in high school, I took a World Religions class that absolutely rocked my world. Our teacher was a young, smart and quirky man who had himself spent a good portion of his life searching for spiritual truth in the world's various religions. He presented each religion with great care and accuracy and often involved students who practiced the faith to help lead and direct the discussions. He was very affirming of my fundamentalist Baptist faith commitment, though he himself was a progressive Christian. He did his best to avoid undermining his students' faith or causing any doubts about the validity of their beliefs, not because he was afraid of the backlash from parents but because he genuinely wanted to help his students embrace their own religious tradition. He was an extraordinary man.

As I sat through his class every day, I found myself amazed that at the core of every religious tradition, there seemed to be beliefs and values that aligned with mine. Many of the religions we learned about had similar ideas and practices that seemed to complement my Christian faith in unexpected ways. In my head, I tried to justify the similarities by telling myself that even the most false religions still contain a kernel of truth, even if everything else was still wrong. The more I tried to write off my intrigue with other religions, the more compelled I felt to explore them. There was something inside me, a deep yearning to learn more and experience God in fresh ways. As I listened to lesson after lesson on the various world religions I found myself drawn to many of the Eastern Traditions – Buddhism, Hinduism, and Taoism – but felt 'dirty' for being interested in these 'false religions'. I was convinced that my fundamentalist Christian faith was the path that led to absolute truth and a right relationship with God. This meant that every other belief or idea that did not align with our interpretation of the Bible was a false teaching and ultimately damnable. I believed that. I felt that I *had* to believe that. To hold to anything less solid would be to water down my faith and sell out to the ways of the world. No other denomination or religious tradition could possibly benefit me and certainly wouldn't lead me to know the Truth. I repeated that mantra to myself often. But the problem was that as I studied, read, and listened to people present these alternative religions, my heart seemed to burn within me.

It became harder for me to simply write off my peers' beliefs as 'false teachings', especially when so many of them mirrored my own beliefs. Something began to happen. The more intrigued in other religions I became, the more I found myself beginning to question the validity of my own faith. Did we really have all the right answers? Could our understanding of God truly be the only right understanding? But I kept these struggles to myself.

Over the next few years as I moved to Chicago for college, my faith got a whole lot messier. Late night theology conversations in my dormitory provoked me to rethink a number of beliefs that I had simply accepted without critically engaging with them. The experience of interacting with a variety of people from different Christian and non-Christian spiritual traditions continued to challenge my presuppositions about every aspect of my life. By the end of my sophomore year in college, the faith that I had once held to so firmly had become like sand, spilling through my fingers as I desperately tried to hold on to it. The black and white answers had all but vanished and a new world of grey opened up around me. The theological labels I once claimed with so much pride became meaningless. I began to realise that so much of what I had taken for granted was not as clear-cut as I had once thought. When these realisations began to emerge, I suddenly realised that I had an important choice to make. I could either reject these doubts as sinful and wrong or I could listen to them and seek God's guidance as I explored their implications. I desperately wanted to choose the first option. I tried to ignore and even combat the doubts and new ways of thinking. But the more I fought, the louder their voices became.

One day my friend John burst into my dorm room after his first philosophy class. He dropped his backpack on the floor and plopped down on my futon. I could tell that he was flustered. He looked at me straight in the eyes. 'Brandan,' he said, 'I don't know what's happening to me. Dr Wheeler just blew up everything I ever thought I believed. I don't think I can be a Calvinist anymore. In fact, I think I may be … post-modern.' He said this with a nervous grin on his face. He seemed to be relieved, and I didn't understand why. 'Not a Calvinist? Post-modern? What in the world? How could this even be possible?!' I retorted. Immediately I opened my browser to Google and typed in, 'Why a Christian can't be post-modern' and began reading off lines from apologetics articles, desperately trying to shake him out of this 'dangerous' haze. Instead of engaging in debate with me, John stood up and placed a book on my desk. The book was called *How Postmodernism Serves (My) Faith*[1] and he told me to take some time to read it over. As he left my room, I sat motionless in my desk chair, simultaneously sensing a great deal of anxiety and a little bit of excitement rush over me. Anxiety because I had been warned for years about the danger of post-modernism. Excitement because I knew that the same impulses that led John to begin asking questions about his faith were the same ones that I had been wrestling with for a few months. Now, I too was beginning to feel … liberated. I wasn't alone in my doubts. John had questions too. I wasn't sure where this was heading and I wasn't sure what to do. So I opened the book and began to read.

For years, I had rejected these kinds of thoughts, believing that they were tools of the Devil meant to pull me away from my faith in Jesus. Instead of exploring the depths of my questions, I clung tightly to the answers that I had been heard from my pastors. I believed that my salvation was based on the correctness of my theology. I had come to believe that the only way to be in right standing with God was to have a correct understanding of what I considered 'core doctrines' – beliefs ranging from literal, six-day creation to the penal-substitutionary death of Jesus on the cross. I had come to understand that if someone didn't understand these doctrines in a satisfactory manner then they could not be truly 'saved'. When this is your understanding of salvation, questions and doubts become the ultimate enemy of faith.

---

1 *How Postmodernism Serves (My) Faith* by Crystal Downing, Intervarsity Press

But at this point, suppressing my doubts just seemed radically dishonest. If my salvation was truly linked to my 'correct theology' then I certainly wasn't fooling God. He knew about my questions. And now that I knew I wasn't alone in my wanderings, I felt like I could finally begin asking the questions that I had suppressed for so long.

It was experiences like these that sparked my initial desire to explore beyond the strictly defined boundaries of my faith. This impulse was rooted in my all-consuming desire to know God and to represent him rightly in the world. But this sort of 'seeking' isn't always seen as a valuable exercise in many Christian communities. I had long been taught that I must resist and reject all forms of doubt or anything that would obscure the 'clear teaching of the Bible.' I had been assured that I had been taught the singular way to salvation and the only right way to view the world, so that all other exploration was futile. When people would criticise me for being closed-minded, my pastor taught me the surefire comeback – 'It's not that I'm closed minded, it's that I have already found the answer!' I would say confidently with a grin on my face. But underneath this mask of confidence and certainty was someone who had real questions and struggles with so much of what he had come to believe. The tension between acting confidently and knowing deep down that I really didn't 'know' what I said I knew caused me a great deal of anxiety. But now that I was on my own for the first time and was surrounded by friends who also reluctantly began to admit their doubts and struggles, I felt free to begin exploring. And once the floodgate was opened, it was impossible to shut it.

There are many topics that Christians simply assume to be the absolute and clear teaching of the Bible and therefore they give them little thought before professing wholehearted belief in them. As I became comfortable asking questions and confronting my doubts, I started to understand just how many things I had taken for granted.

How many of us have found ourselves reading the Bible and coming across a verse that seems really out of place or contradictory? I had been taught to view any contradiction or 'error' in the Bible as only an *apparent* contradiction or error, having the appearance of an imperfection but actually being harmonious or in line with my theology. But what if these contradictions and imperfections were real and actually revealed something profound about the Scriptures? This was a thought that I never felt safe entertaining. And what about the issue of God's sovereignty? I had been fully persuaded that the Bible upheld a generally Calvinistic theology, but when I began to reexamine the Bible with open eyes, I began to see that everything wasn't as clear as it seemed. There was nuance and colour, tension and even paradox. Before these experiences, I would have seen such a thought as inherently 'sinful', but now I was beginning to find that when I could approach God and the Bible with honesty and openness, embracing the wide array of perspectives believing that each contained a valid kernel of truth, I began to see the world with fresh eyes.

When we are able to systematise and theologise God down to a set of absolute theological principles, I believe that we lose something essential. When our faith becomes nothing more than a stagnant creed or unchanging statement of belief, we lose sight of the majesty and glory of God, the mystery and diversity that gives vibrancy to our faith. Whenever we speak about God or the subjects related to the Divine, we must work hard to remain humble. As finite human beings, every attempt we make to speak of God falls dramatically short of the Reality that is. Even though I believe that we are able to interact with and have an indescribably deep and personal relationship with God, the truth is that every experience we have, belief we profess, or fact we embrace is filtered through our heart and minds, which tints our perspective and fogs up our glasses. The moment we begin to believe we have got something about God figured out with certainty is the moment we can be sure we are no longer speaking about God. Or as St

Augustine once said, '*We are talking about God. What wonder is it that you do not understand? If you do understand, then it is not God.*'

Does this mean that there is no such things absolute truth? Did reading a book on postmodernism simply make me a flimsy relativist with no backbone? Absolutely not. (Unless you feel comfortable calling St Augustine a postmodern relativist.) I am not saying that we cannot know Truth, of course we can. But what I am suggesting is that Truth isn't a set of absolute propositions; rather, it is a person. Jesus Christ. He is Truth and like all people, he is dynamic. He cannot be classified, systematised, and organised into neat little boxes and categories. He defies boundaries and descriptions. And if Jesus is the visible image of the invisible God, as the Apostle Paul claims, then we must assume that God is just as dynamic. God is not a lifeless rock, but a wild, untamed lion. God is the grand Artist of Eternity, filled with passion, desire, and creative energy. God cannot be reduced to a set of attributes. God cannot be accurately described by even the most eloquent of words. When we are talking about God, we're simply doing the best we can to describe that Reality that upholds our Universe.

C.S. Lewis is perhaps one of the greatest theologians the Church has ever seen. All of his works, whether theological, philosophical, fictitious, or poetic, pulsate with some of the richest and yet most accessible theology that has ever been written. Lewis was well aware that all his writings, thoughts, and even prayers about God would ultimately fall dreadfully short of reality. He recognised that there was very little certainty, very little black and white, involved in the art of theology and the Christian life.

One of the places he most clearly articulated this perspective is in a short poem he penned entitled 'A Footnote to All Prayer'. In the poem, he writes that all of our prayers 'blaspheme' if taken at their literal words, and prays that God in his 'magnetic mercy' would divert our 'unskillfully aimed arrows' and 'limping metaphors' and receive them based upon our intentions and not the words' 'literal sense', which always will fall short.

Oh, that modern day theologians would embrace such epistemological humility! What would our spiritual lives look like if we began all of our prayers like this?[2] Confessing to God that all the words we speak are merely shadows of Reality, and yet deeply knowing that God's grace covers and translates our inaccurate speech. How liberating it is to know that no one truly has all of the answers, and that it's actually supposed to be that way.

When I began to discover the vast amount of grey in my once black and white world, the amount of weight that was lifted off my soul was unbelievable. When I understood that everything didn't have cut-and-dried answers, that theology was a complex and imprecise art, and that God himself was dynamic and filled with colour and tension, I began to finally feel ... safe. Safe, in the sense that I now had come to realise that God was not going to judge me based on the correctness of my beliefs. I was now confident that none of us had the 'correct theology'; instead, each of us was just doing the best we could to be faithful in describing the God that we knew. Sure, there were some common beliefs that millions of my fellow Christians had agreed on as fundamental throughout the ages, and they were there to serve as guard rails on our theological journey. But even they are just our best finite attempts to describe the infinite One.

As we journey throughout our spiritual lives, we will often be tempted to settle into one theological perspective and claim it as our resting place. But to do so prevents us from exploration and discovery, which is the very purpose of our lives. We live in a world that is truly enchanted, and the Spirit that creates and sustains all things has heights and depths that defy our wildest imaginations. Eternity is our endless exploration of God. We shall never reach the end of who he is or what he can do. The deeper we probe, the more colour and variation we will find. This is what it means to be a nomad. One who is never content with simply settling down. One who always yearns to know what lies just beyond the

2 To read this entire poem, visit http://www.mbird.com/2012/03/c-s-lewis-footnote-to-all-prayers

next hill. When we realise that the purpose of our life is not to find and comprehend absolute Truth but rather to explore the tension and mystery at the heart of all things, we are set free to go where no one has gone before, to expand our boundaries, and to discover the new things that God is doing all around us with joy and expectation instead of fear and apprehension.

7

Experience

God, according to all the great spiritual traditions,
cannot be comprehended by the finite mind
but can nevertheless be known in an
intimate encounter with his presence.

David Bentley Hart

If you haven't figured it out already, religious people *really* like to be right. I know, because for most of my short faith journey, I understood that to be faithful to God was to have all of the correct answers to all of life's most complex questions. At twelve years old, I could tell you exactly how the universe was created and describe in detail what the afterlife was going to look like. These things weren't merely my 'beliefs' either. I knew them for sure. I had learned them directly from the source of all truth, the Bible, and no matter what evidence or opinions you proposed to me, I knew that I was right and you were wrong. God was on my side, and I was just telling you exactly what his word said. And as my Pastor always used to preach, 'God said it, I believe it, and that settles it!' But even for the most devout fundamentalist, sometimes knowing all of the right answers isn't enough to fill the void in our souls. Sometimes, at the end of the day, a set of propositions just doesn't ease the anxiety in our hearts. Sometimes, believing a systematic theology fails to provide the guidance that we need in our lives.

In many Christian traditions, the path to salvation is paved by bricks of truth. As we accept one truth claim, we are led to the next, each factor leading us closer to salvation. This method of spirituality works for many in our post-Enlightenment world. Much of Christian thinking has been dominated by this idea that if only we can nail down the right theology, confess the right creeds, take the right social views, then our lives will find fulfilment and meaning. We will be connected to God. This is the message that many young Christians are taught to believe. If it doesn't come directly from the mouth of the preachers, it is demonstrated by the way our community reacts to those with whom we disagree.

But what happens when our truth claims are challenged? What happens when we sit in our high school biology class and learn about the theory of Evolution and it seems to disprove all that we had been taught about the creation of the world from the book of Genesis in Sunday School? As we've already explored, if our faith is rooted in believing the right theology, then we have the choice to either reject the new knowledge being presented to us by our Biology teacher, or we must reject our faith, which is to ultimately reject salvation.

I have grown up in one of the most interconnected and educated generations in the history of the world, and it is this naiveté and ignorance that causes so many young people to be opposed to faith. Living in a community where we are told that our very belonging is contingent upon whether or not we agree with all of the right doctrines and dogmas is totally uninteresting and unrealistic. Instead of cultivating the abundant life that Jesus talks about, this type of thinking quenches the Spirit of curiosity, which is the very spirit of faith that resides in the hearts of those who seek after God.

We are warned that if we were to begin to question even one of the bricks that make up the path to salvation, the whole path would come undone. We are told to confess and affirm, rather than to critically think, engage, or seek after a personal experience with God. Many are even told that desiring to experience God instead of mentally assenting to his existence is somehow sinful and untrustworthy, justified with out of context quotes like this one from the Book of Jeremiah 17:9: *'The heart is deceitful above all things, and desperately sick; who can understand it?'*

And yet, the very people who make such claims are the same people who emphasise the importance of the born-again experience, that moment when we encounter Jesus Christ in an emotional and experiential way that radically transforms our lives and ignites faith in our hearts. The same type of experience that changed the life of the apostle Paul on the road to Damascus. The experience of the earliest Christians in the book of Acts, who encountered the Spirit of God in a way that far surpassed merely affirming truth claims about the resurrection of Christ. No, they experienced the Spirit of living Christ in their day-to-day lives. Why, then, do so many people today not only lack an experiential encounter with God, but also actually condemn such desires?

A few years back, I found myself in a spiritual dry spell. One of those seasons where you try your hardest to pray, but can't help but feel that your words are hitting off the ceiling and bouncing back to you. I tried my hardest to sense God's closeness, I tried reaffirming the 'truths' I believed, hoping that they could sustain me in this period of Divine disconnectedness. On the surface, I was doing everything that I had always been taught to do, but it still didn't feel like enough. I talked to some mentors about this feeling, and was reminded that my problem was not disconnection from God, but rather my fleshly pursuit of an experience over belief in truth. While this reassured me for a period of time, I eventually found myself deeply distressed. Here I was, spending all of this time seeking to know God in my head, when all that I really desired was to *feel* his presence in my heart. I began to wonder if the disconnection I felt from God was a direct result of how I was viewing my relationship with him.

I remembered the words of Scripture in James 4:12 (NIrV), *'You don't have what you want, because you don't ask God.'* Maybe the reason that I wasn't experiencing God was because I was never actually expecting God to show up in any real, tangible way. I had always been afraid to desire such a thing. Experience, emotions, and feelings are all viewed as generally negative things in much of the religious world. Yet at the same time, I knew that the pages of Scripture are filled with stories of God showing up in very real, tangible, and experiential ways. I continued to skim through the Bible, reading of the many ways in which people have radically encountered God throughout the ages.

We can look to the Prophets, who heard the voice of God and had vivid visions of his glory. We can read about the monarchs and rulers who argued and conversed with God. And we can look at Jesus, who undoubtedly had a deep, intimate, and experiential relationship with the Father. Time and time again, we find Jesus fleeing the crowds of people who followed after him to spend time communing with God in prayer and meditation. Jesus, though a Rabbi who had great respect for the word of God, seemed to clearly value loving God *experientially* and loving his neighbour *tangibly* above theological certitude. In fact, as we've already seen, Jesus consistently finds himself in conflict with the Pharisees, a hyper-orthodox, Scripture-centred group of religious leaders who, like many Christians today, valued theological accuracy and moral purity over an intimate relationship with God. Jesus' lax take on Judaism in favour of living in communion with God and his neighbour often infuriated the Pharisees and other religious leaders. Jesus was supposed to be *one* of them. He was supposed to have believed and practiced the same things that they did. But instead of being devoted to his religious tradition, Jesus devoted himself to knowing God, which, it turned out, were two radically different things.

As I looked at the pages of Scripture, I realised that I had aligned myself with the religion of the Pharisees instead of the spirituality of Christ. I had been trying to commune with God through mental assent to doctrines and the affirmation of creeds rather than through direct connection with the God in whom I live and move and have my being. I knew that God was as close to me as my very breath, but I had never really experienced that. Or at least, I hadn't for a very long time. I desired to feel the connection and experience that I saw so many others had throughout the Scripture. I wanted to know God beyond mere knowledge. I needed to sense God. To see him or hear him or feel him. Believing in his existence was no longer enough to sustain me.

I began to research Christian spirituality through the ages, looking deeper into some of the spiritual practices of the other denominations that I had visited during my church search in Chicago. The more I studied, the more I became amazed at the vast mystical and charismatic traditions that existed within nearly every stream of Christianity. I read about the monastic orders of the Roman Catholic Church and the meditation and contemplative practices of Eastern Orthodoxy. I dug deeper into the Pentecostal tradition to learn about the more charismatic practices that led people to encounter God. The more I studied, the more I realised just how far Western Christianity has moved away from her experiential roots. Some of the earliest writings of Christianity are deeply mystical texts, outlining very real supernatural encounters with God. There was very little systematic theology and whole lot of being led by the Spirit. An idea that will cause the average modern Christian to shrink back in scepticism.

But the early Christians' spirituality was far more than reading the Bible and praying every day. It was deeply rhythmic; a well-structured pattern of living that ensured a person would remain aware and connected to the presence of God throughout the day. Many traditions involved some form of meditation. Others involved chanting, pilgrimage, fasting, praying, walking labyrinths, and many other strategies to centre one's self and connect with God. Whether they made use of simple mantras or prayer beads, whether repeated liturgical prayers or ecstatically spoke in tongues, the earliest followers of Christ knew God in a profoundly real way. They felt God at the core of their being. It was this deep knowing that emboldened them to be able to stand firm in their faith even in the most tumultuous of times. When they stood before crowds of people gathered in the Colosseum in Rome preparing to be martyred, they stood there not defending 'truth claims' or a set of religious doctrines. They instead stood unable to deny the God they intimately knew and experienced. Only when one has known and communed with God will they be convicted enough to give their lives for him.

But the Church today has moved far away from putting such an emphasis on personal experience as the basis for one's relationship with God. The fear is that such an idea sets a trajectory for subjectivity when it comes to weightier matters of doctrine and theology, which would lead a community into total chaos. If our faith was more focused on 'feelings' than it was on the clear truth communicated through the Bible, what would be our foundation? How could we say with certainty that something was right and something else was wrong? These questions are at the heart of the movement away from mystical and charismatic forms of spirituality and I believe are one of the key reasons that many people are walking away from faith altogether.

While it is true that the foundation of our faith goes far beyond whether or not we happen to 'feel' God at any given moment, if we try to build our entire spirituality apart from seeking to know God in a experiential way, we are inevitably setting ourselves up for failure. Many young people grew up in families that instructed them in the doctrines of the Christian faith. For their entire childhood, they may be able to accept these things as true and allow them to shape the way they view the world. But eventually, there comes a point when knowing about God isn't enough. There comes a point when we need to sense God. We need to know beyond knowledge that there is a God who loves us and is with us. If our tradition tells us that this desire is sinful or immature, and offers us no direction on how to spiritually seek such an experience with God, than it is understandable that many would simply walk away from faith altogether. If Christianity has nothing more to offer than a set of religious doctrines and a worldview, then it has nothing compelling to offer. There are many religions that offer more appealing worldviews and other spiritual paths that bring more sensory pleasure that we could affiliate with. Or else, we could leave behind religion altogether, believing that all of it is about indoctrination and vying for cultural power, which is the very place in which many former Christians find themselves every day.

Knowledge just isn't enough. It's not enough to sustain our faith. It's not enough to enrich our lives. Human beings are fundamentally wired for sensory experience. In any of our other relationships, we expect to engage many of our senses. That's how we grow closer. That's how we enhance our relationships. We snuggle with our parents. We wrestle with our siblings. We hug our friends. We shake hands with our co-workers. We kiss our partner. All of these physical actions create tangible experiences that bind us closer to one another and form a depth in our relationships that often goes beyond description. No matter what I may know about a friend, it is the experiences we share that make up our relationship. No matter how bad a fight I may get into with my parents, I will always come around, because our relationship has been formed on the basis of a deep, experiential intimacy that cannot be affected by temporal circumstances. Likewise, if our spiritual tradition doesn't lead us to a regular experience with God, then any temporal circumstance can deal a tremendous blow to our faith. But when we do cultivate a deep relationship with God through practices and disciplines, than our faith is bolstered and our lives are enhanced. Because that's how humans were created.

Many people of my generation are rediscovering the mystical and charismatic traditions within Christianity. After growing up in a Western society that emphasises empirical, scientific truth over intuitive and experiential knowing, we have grown tired and cynical of the cold hard 'truth' of religion. Many of us have begun to identify as 'spiritual but not religious', which is used to say that we appreciate and see value in the experience of spirituality, but find little use for the structures, systems, and dogmas of organised religion. We are seeking traditions and practices that keep us rooted in God but allow us the freedom to wander, seek, and search for the path which most resonates with our soul.

In my journey to experience God, I have found great resonance in the contemplative traditions of the Franciscans. I discovered this tradition when I visited a monastery in Chicago for a weekend. When I arrived, a gentle elderly man, dressed in a long brown robe, greeted me. He brought me into the main room of the monastery where a number of the monks had gathered and were sitting silently, waiting to begin meditation. I sat in the back of the room, unsure of what I was about to experience. As I said before, I had believed that these contemplative practices were actually incredibly dangerous for the Christian, but I sceptically followed along with the prompts that the leading monk spoke. We sat silently, first, and began to repeat a prayer with one another. We prayed, 'Lord Jesus Christ, Son of God, have mercy on me a sinner.' As we each softly chanted this prayer, I was taken aback by the Christ-centredness of what I was experiencing. I later learned that the prayer we were repeating was known as *The Jesus Prayer* and the practice of repeating this prayer during meditation dated back to ancient group of Christian mystics known as the Desert Fathers of the fifth century. We continued repeating this mantra for another ten minutes, and then a gong was sounded. The room then fell silent and we were instructed that we were to begin a thirty-minute period of silent meditation.

As I closed my eyes, my mind immediately began to fill with thoughts. The leader told us that as thoughts came in to our minds, we were not to engage them or judge them, but rather to let them pass. If they became too distracting, we could refocus ourselves by repeating the word 'Maranatha'. I sat pensively, trying to focus my mind on the word 'Marantha' and to clear my thoughts. Immediately, I felt sensations all over my body. I itched and ached and desperately wanted to move. I was astounded at the amount of resistance my mind and body were giving to this practice. But I pressed forward, determined to make it through the entire period. After about ten minutes of intense internal struggle, I finally got to a place of inner stillness and peace. I was astounded at just how hard it was to meditate, but also how at peace I truly felt when I actually got to a place of quietness. The next twenty minutes flew by quickly, as I sat in a warmth and stillness that I had never felt before. As the gong sounded at the thirty-minute mark, we slowly opened our eyes and together spoke the words of *The Lord's Prayer.* As we began, there was a tangible sense of interconnectedness and the presence of God in the room. Goosebumps formed on my neck and arms as we prayed these ancient words with one another. Our words seemed to sync with stunning precision and a powerful sense that God was in and with us.

As we ended the time of corporate meditation, I slowly made my way back to my room. I was surprised at just how effective my experience with meditation had been. Throughout the course of the next two days of my retreat, I began reading some ancient spiritual texts that had been provided in my room. All of the practices that I read about had deep roots in Scripture and had a clear focus on Christ. I experimented with a plethora of new spiritual disciplines, from *Lectio Divina,* a meditative way of reading Scripture and seeking the Spirit's illumination, to walking the prayer labyrinth, a maze of sorts that is used to help focus our prayer and meditation as we journey from the edge to the centre of the maze. With each new practice came a new experience. Some were completely unhelpful. Others connected me to God in a deep way.

As I emerged from the weekend in the monastery, I felt a sense of spiritual rejuvenation that I hadn't felt in a long time. I knew that I had encountered God over the course of my retreat and I knew that these 'taboo' practices had helped me foster that connection.

Over the coming months, I continued to practice meditation and began joining other young Christians around Chicago for different contemplative gatherings. I discovered that there was a growing sense among many of my peers that the gnostic version of Christianity with which we we had grown up was no longer working, and many of us had set out on a journey to discover new ways of cultivating a relationship with God. I found that the more I practised a wide array of spiritual disciplines, the more sensitive and aware I became to the presence of God all around me. My faith began to grow as my theology and doctrine became supported by my regular encounters with God.

While it is true that experience alone is not enough to sustain our lives, it is a major part of what it means to be a human. We should value theology and doctrine as faithful guides along the way, helping us to put language to the indescribable Reality that we find ourselves encountering. But when our theology and language fall short, as they always do, it is our experiential knowledge of God that will ultimately sustain us. As spiritual nomads with an insatiable desire to delve deeper into the depths of the great mysteries of our Universe, we must learn to seek and sense the presence of God. If our faith and indeed our lives are going to flourish, we must discover the ways in which we best connect with God and prioritise them in our lives. Not everyone will resonate with contemplative spirituality. Not everyone will enjoy charismatic worship. But each and every one of us must do our best to seek a deep knowledge of God that goes beyond our intellect and touches the depths of our soul. God is always reaching out to us with extended arms, ready to reveal himself to us. But we must find the way that opens our spiritual eyes and allows us to gaze at his glory. For when we can finally stand in the presence of God, our lives will be changed. And we don't have to wait until 'heaven'. God is here with us now. Can you sense him?

8

Roots

Change your opinions, keep your principles;
Change your leaves, keep intact your roots.

Victor Hugo

Growing up, my family never really had any 'traditions'. Other than gathering the extended family together once or twice a year for major holidays, there were no real rituals or practices we engaged in that connected us to our ancestors. In fact, there was never really any talk about our ancestors. I'm not sure my parents really knew much about where they came from beyond their own grandparents. On the whole, many millennials have had a similar experience growing up. Many of us grew up devoid of tradition or a broad narrative in which to place ourselves. Most of us didn't participate in small traditional practices like gathering around a common table for dinner each evening. Most of us can only vaguely begin to tell you about our family heritage, listing the eight or nine countries we think we heard our parents say we had ancestors in. That is usually the extent of our connectedness to our families' past.

Part of the modern opposition to tradition began after the Enlightenment era, when the Western world as a whole became so focused on innovation and the future that we began to decentralise the importance of remaining connected to the traditions of the past. Every major societal institution from the family, to schools, to churches began to become so focused on being innovative and relevant that they failed to recognise the importance of remembering and honouring our roots. Soon, apathy regarding tradition turned into total opposition to any form of traditional thinking or practice. In Christianity, churches of all denominational stripes began to completely do away with things such as liturgies, stories, and ritual practices, seeing them as hindrances to their progression into the twenty-first century. It was this reactionary mindset that caused many modern institutions to be so opposed to tradition. Little did we know that when we disconnected from our past, we would create a crisis of identity for coming generations.

Without being connected to a lineage of people, stories, rituals, and values, a deep void has been opened up in my soul. From a very early age, I found myself reflecting on my purpose in life and the point of it all. Whereas young people of the past could find guidance with these deep questions of the soul, because I had little to ground myself in, I was sent on a wild goose chase for meaning and purpose. Perhaps one of the reasons I, and many in my generation, have become wanderers, is because of this fundamental lack of a foundation on which to move about the world. Now, I am not suggesting that our unrootedness is either good or bad – for such a thing cannot be labeled morally. In many ways, we have been uniquely set up to innovate and discover in ways previous generations have not. On the other hand, it could be argued that without a narrative within which to place our lives, we may lack perspective and a sense of responsibility or legacy.

When I realised this lack of rootedness, I became fascinated with both my family's heritage and the ancient traditions of the Church. I began digging around the internet, searching for information about my past as both a Robertson and as a Christian, and began to discover the compelling ancient stories of both. The Robertsons, it turned out, were one of the oldest clans in

Scotland. My heritage was filled with kings and princes who ruled the Highlands. I also discovered perhaps the greatest treasure of my heritage - Celtic music. As I started listening to the music of my ancestors, I felt as if the melodies and lyrics gave voice to deepest desires of my soul. (I know that might sound overly cheesy, but it's the truth.) As I continued to delve deeper into my Celtic heritage, small and scattered parts of my life began to make sense. I realised that I was a part of something much larger than myself. I began to feel like I had a tribe I belonged to.

Similarly, as a new Christian, I began examining the writings of the Church Fathers, such as *The Didache* (or '*The Teaching*') that laid out in detail the lives of the earliest followers of Christ. To my surprise, I discovered many of the practices I had heard preachers scoff at as excessive and superfluous had their roots in the most ancient versions of our faith. I learned that the early Christians lived disciplined lives of prayer and worship, setting aside five scheduled prayer times a day. They had a liturgy they followed for worship that was rooted in the ancient Jewish liturgies used in the synagogues, connecting this new fledgling faith to our Hebrew origins. The early Christians practiced communion or the *Eucharist* (from the Greek word meaning 'to give thanks') regularly, and to them, it seemed it was much more than a time of remembrance. This ritual held great power, and was the very centre of early Christian life and practice. I was mystified by the many foreign practices of the early Christian community. Why had we done away with them? The faith that I read about in these ancient writings was so foreign. It had so much depth and mystery. It was filled with symbols and rhythms that helped those early followers of Christ live into the Gospel narrative each and every day of their lives.

As I began to gain a sense of meaning from understanding the stories and practices of my past, I also began searching for ways to live in light of what I had come to discover. As a Protestant Evangelical, this of course led me to begin examining the Roman Catholic and Eastern Orthodox Churches. These denominations offered something that no Evangelical church I knew of could – a true connection to the rhythms and traditions of the past. Both churches were filled with different aspects and practices of our faith throughout the ages. I remember the awe that came over me when I entered into the dark sanctuary of the Eastern Orthodox Church that was directly across the street from my Bible college. Icons lined the walls, incense ascended to the ceiling and fell, forming a mysterious haze. There were no pews, except for a few that lined the walls for newcomers and the elderly. The priest emerged with a long beard, dressed in elaborate robes, reminding me of Mr Tumnus the Fawn from *The Chronicles of Narnia*. Though the whole service was completely foreign to me, I was strangely comfortable and almost familiar with everything that was going on. It was like these Christians were taking their cues directly from the writings of the early Church. As it turned out, they were.

The best (and funniest) part of the Orthodox service came when it was time to take communion. Everyone in the sanctuary got into a line to proceed up to the priest who fed both the bread and the wine to each person on a long golden spoon. I wasn't sure what exactly the procedure was, or who was able to receive communion in the Orthodox church, so I made my friend Troy get in line in front of me. I figured he could look like the ignorant Protestant and I could play smart after seeing how he did it. As Troy approached the priest, I stepped up behind him. The priest leaned forward and asked Troy, 'Are you Orthodox?' Troy looked back at me and I nodded my head. 'Of course we're orthodox,' I whispered to Troy. We were Bible college students after all. Who could be *more* theologically orthodox than us? The priest leaned in and said, 'No, no, I mean, are you baptised into the *Eastern* Orthodox Church?' We both shook our heads in shame. The priest, seeing our embarrassment, consoled us and instructed us to stick around to talk with him after the service concluded. After the service has ended, the priest came over to us with a grin on his face. 'Y'all are from Moody, right?' he asked. It turned out that it was a very common occurrence for curious Evangelicals from my college to wander across the street into the Orthodox Church, and Father Michael had become quite used to graciously turning unknowing students away from communion.

This awkward experience only intensified my hunger to know more about these beautiful ancient traditions. I began to discover that the Christian tradition was laden with rich rituals and practices that gave a depth to our faith I never knew existed. I continued to attend various Orthodox, Episcopal, and Catholic churches around Chicago and read anything and everything I could get my hands on about Christian tradition, liturgy, and rituals. I learned of things like the Church Calendar, a year-long rhythm that rooted believers in the Gospel story every week throughout the year. In many Christian traditions, Rules of Living were created to help establish a rhythm that ensured an individual would spend time throughout their day praying and meditating, keeping life centred in God. I discovered prayer books, filled with some of the most poetic and beautiful supplications I had ever heard, dating back thousands of years. As I prayed these beautiful prayers and attempted to live into the rhythm of the Church Calendar, I felt a profound sense of connectedness to the One Holy Catholic Church through the ages. For the first time, I began to feel like I belonged to a family of Saints. Beyond my independent Evangelical megachurch, I realised I was part of something much bigger. God's work on earth extended far beyond the contemporary worship songs and celebrity pastors. I realised we are simply the current actors on the stage of God's grand drama, preceded by a long line of devout men and women who, like us, tried to be faithful to the way of Jesus in the best way they knew how.

The individualism that has been propagated in modern Christianity has done great harm to our sense of collective responsibility. We have been told to focus on 'reading the Bible for ourselves,' 'cultivating our own spiritual walk,' and 'maintaining a personal relationship with God'. And while all of these things have their place, we have lost the sense of corporate identity and forgotten the value of family and tradition. When the earliest Christians called each other brother, sister, father, or mother, they meant it. There was a deeply felt sense of interrelatedness to all followers of Christ, a connection that rivaled that of blood relatives. When someone was baptised into the Body of Christ, they were adopted into an actual family. They received the new family name and became an inheritor of, and participant in, a long rich spiritual and cultural tradition. This sense of family identity and rootedness helped to ground believers in the faith handed down to them, and gave them a framework and story to pass down to other generations as well.

In the churches I grew up in, there was absolutely no sense of tradition or a broader narrative we participated in. Instead, we focused on our communities' autonomy and God's unique work in our midst. We were rarely connected to other churches in the area because all of us were focused on creating our own unique style and brand of Christianity. While many creative innovations have come out of such communities, the fact is that these churches ultimately left me feeling disconnected and lost within the choppy waters of life. Not because these churches didn't have great social groups and communities, but because the spirituality I learned had no significant track record. Our spiritual practices, like reading the Bible and singing the latest 'Hillsong' hit, were distinctly modern. I couldn't find Biblical examples of them. And when they ceased being effective methods of connecting me to God and stoking the flames of my spiritual life, I was left wondering if my faith had any relevance or value.

During my freshman year in Bible college, I spent hours upon hours praying and reading the Bible, only to walk away feeling more disconnected to God than ever before. In Evangelical Christianity, these were the only two 'spiritual practices' I'd ever been taught, and when they began to fail, I found myself turning to explore and discover the wealth of traditions, spiritualities, and practices that existed within Christianity through visiting various churches around Chicago. As I began to study why the Eastern Orthodox Church practiced their faith the way they did, I discovered a treasure trove of spiritual writings that dated back to the time of Christ. Often, the authors of these writings described similar struggles to the ones I was facing in my spiritual life and recounted methods and practices that had been passed down to them from previous generations of saints who struggled in similar ways. From there, I began reading Roman Catholic and Anglican writings, and discovered the rich spiritual tradition of my ancestors in Scotland and Ireland through the writings of the Celtic Christians.

Before I began my own personal study of these traditions, I had only heard negative things about them from my non-traditional community. Rituals and traditions were seen as stumbling blocks to a true relationship with God, which was meant to be intensely personal and autonomous. But, as with so many other areas of my faith, as I began to explore beyond the boundaries I had been taught, I discovered a vast new world of writings, traditions, and practices that helped me root my faith and my life in something much larger than myself.

The more I learned about them, the more interested I became in those expressions of Christianity that were steeped in liturgy and tradition. I personally became fascinated with the Anglican tradition which was deeply Protestant and even Evangelical, but still remained connected to the long, ancient flow of Christianity. The Anglican liturgy provided a richly theological, deeply contemplative space for me to recharge and reconnect with God every week. Beyond the flashing lights and vibrating sound systems of the typical Evangelical church, here I found a place to truly connect with God with my heart and mind. And though the experience was deeply personal, for the first time, I experienced God in a profoundly communal sense. When the entire congregation came together to confess our sins, we did so in unison, kneeling down, one next to the other, and reciting ancient words that Christians all around the world had been using to find forgiveness for centuries. When we confessed the Apostles' Creed, we did so as one people, with all of our various doubts and questions, relying on the faith of our neighbour to support us in our confession of these ancient tenets. For the first time, I experienced the church as the one Body of Christ. We moved together. We sang together. We prayed together. And every week, we joined each other at the altar, kneeling to receive the body and blood of Christ, which united us all together in a profoundly real and mysterious sense.

As I continued to attend the Anglican church (while also occasionally sneaking into a Catholic mass or two on the side), I was surprised to find the people filling the pews around me weren't just few elderly folks who had been Anglican since conception, as I'd expected, but many other young Christians who were also thirsty for getting something more out of their religion. The deeper I dove into studying liturgy and tradition, the more I discovered there was a tremendous interest arising among my peers for the same. We all had come to a point in our lives where we realised our personal faith no longer had the ability to sustain us. We needed to be a part of something stronger than the tingly feeling we got down our spines during a well-played worship song. We needed something more, and that something more was discovered in the midst of an Anglican worship service.

Discovering the roots and rituals of my faith was like discovering my faith for the first time. While I had many valuable and transformative experiences from my Evangelical megachurch days (and still absolutely love a good Hillsong worship set), it was discovering the long lineage that lay behind my faith that became the glue that has held my faith together. Growing up, I never saw the value in traditions and roots. Society had taught me the only thing that mattered was dreaming of and working for a better tomorrow. It was always all about innovation, the next big thing. Rarely did we focus on learning about those who came before us, other than to pass history tests. This post-enlightenment thinking has led to so many fantastic innovations and advancements for our society. Always looking towards tomorrow in hopes of creating a better world has driven humanity to progress faster in science, technology, medicine, justice, and even spirituality than any other period in human history.

But in all of this forward thinking, an inner chasm has been exposed in many people's lives. We cannot merely live for tomorrow. Despite our best efforts, we cannot be truly autonomous beings. We have been created with a primal impulse for connection and meaning, which can only be found when we discover the story of our past. When we understand how we arrived in the world we find ourselves in. When we discover we are connected to an endless line of individuals who have, like us, sought after God in hope of finding redemption and purpose, may we be reminded that in our journey through the never ending deserts of life, we are not alone and tread on well-worn paths of fellow saints and seekers of old. May we find in their stories and practices, wisdom and encouragement for our journeys. And when everything in our lives seems to be blown away by the rushing winds, may we be held firmly in place by our roots, the never- ending thread that connects us to all of the fellow sojourners on this journey called life.

9

Community

*Someone to tell it to is one of
the fundamental needs of human beings.*

Miles Franklin

On this journey of faith, having a place of belonging and a people to walk alongside us are essential. We cannot do life on our own; we weren't created to do it that way. We need fellow sojourners to trek through the valleys and scale the sides of mountains with us. We need people to cheer us on in our challenges, comfort us in our sadness, and celebrate our successes. We need people who will come along with us as we swerve off the straight and narrow, and who are committed to loving us no matter where we may end up. Without this sort of companionship, our lives can become increasingly bleak. When we try to walk the path of our lives on our own, we will inevitably burn out and break down because we are working against our fundamental wiring as humans, created in the image of the relational God.

What I mean by that is, for Christians, our conception of God is fundamentally relational. When we speak of God, we speak of the Trinity. And when we speak of the Trinity, we are speaking of the mystery that God exists in eternal relationship between three individual persons who are yet one substance. For God to be Love, God also has to be in relationship. For what is it to Love without another person? If Love, as defined in the Bible, is self-sacrificial giving for the sake of another, then the Godhead must always have been in relationship with another. It is out of that relationship that Love was birthed. So, according to this ancient doctrine, for all eternity, God has always existed in perfect, loving relationship between Creator, Son, and Holy Spirit. And we are created in that same image. So in order for us to experience Love, we too need to be in relationship. We are wired for it. Despite what some may think, needing others is not a sign of weakness, but the source of strength, health, and vibrancy. According to the Christian story, even God desires community.

I, however, am incredibly independent. I've always been one of those people who absolutely hated group work, and always felt that if you want something done right, you've got to do it yourself. It's not that I think I can actually do things better on my own, but rather that when I'm alone, I can really focus and get things done efficiently. Group work always takes twice as long and you can never be quite sure of the outcome. This mindset has been incredibly helpful at times. It's helped me to accomplish a great many things in my life. But it also is a dangerous mindset. When we become overly independent or self-reliant, we often end up running ourselves off the road and into a ditch. And when you're in a ditch by yourself, it can be incredibly difficult to climb out.

When I began to wander on the edges of Evangelical Christianity, I found it increasingly difficult to commit to a church community. I found myself very uncomfortable in many of the settings that I once valued. My newfound spiritual independence initially resulted in an overinflated ego and a critical spirit. I would sit in the chapel services at my Bible college and critique everything from the worship, to the sermon, to the way people around me engaged in the service. As I sensed I was becoming more 'evolved' and 'enlightened', I began to feel restless in the conservative faith community in which I found myself embedded. This same mindset was not limited to my college, but followed me into church settings on Sundays. I continued to visit churches to try to find a community that was a 'perfect fit' and grew increasingly weary that no such thing could possibly exist. No community seemed to integrate all of the new insights and values I was learning. Most communities were either too conservative and rigid, or else too far left and completely unappealing to me. After months of searching for a community with which to share my faith journey, I decided the only way I'd ever be able to be a part of the perfect church would be if I started my own. As the years went on, my ecclesial arrogance waned. I slowly realised my expectations and critical spirit were unfair and unrealistic, and I couldn't continue to live my life in that space. Nonetheless, I still found it incredibly difficult to find a community with which I felt I could be honest and authentic.

During this season, I began to become incredibly self-reliant and independent with my spirituality. My doubts, questions, and faith became private and personal. I felt if I shared it with others, they would either not understand me or even marginalise me. So, I began to turn inward. I continued to hop between churches every Sunday to fulfil the requirement that my college placed on its students to attend church each week, but I became convinced I would have to travel on my spiritual journey alone.

Because we are spiritual beings, if we decide to internalise our spirituality, we will necessarily internalise our entire life. When we try to live our lives outside of a spiritual community, many of our relationships will begin to wither on the vine. Many of my friends and peers just didn't understand my impulse to continue questioning and exploring, which resulted in a growing chasm between us. This, on top of the fact that I am deeply introverted and have a tendency to be relationally awkward, pushed me into greater isolation and away from any hope of forming a sense of community. Within a few months of living in this sort of isolation, I entered into a place of deep darkness and depression. The pain I felt being alone on my journey was excruciating, leaving me wondering if I should just forget my questions and conform to the faith of my community. Sure, it would be inauthentic, but at least I would have friends to do life with. A community I could call home.

For those of us who identify as nomads, one would think it would be quite easy for us to live our lives completely on the road. There is a real sense of exhilaration and enjoyment when we consider the possible adventures we will have and discoveries we will make as we traverse the never-ending paths that lie before us. But when we try to travel these roads on our own, we are inevitably setting ourselves up for failure and burn out. Humans are intrinsically wired to be in relationship. Our health – spiritually, physically, and psychologically – requires that we live in community with other people. Though many of us may find ourselves in a place where we feel like *no one* understands our struggle and *no church* could ever be a comfortable fit for us, it is essential to intentionally commit to a community and to relationships, no matter how much tension or discomfort there may be. Relationships are complex and messy. There will be pain and conflict. People will misunderstand us and criticise us for the way we live our lives. But none of that can compare to the pain that we will experience when we isolate ourselves from relationships.

In the early days of the Church, as this new fledgling movement of Jesus' followers had just set out on the journey of following after God's Spirit in this new thing he was doing in their midst, they recognised the importance of being in community. When you read through the Book of Acts, you discover that even in the midst of great theological diversity and disagreement about what it looked like to be a Christian, the early disciples were committed to walking through life together. They were united, not by their understanding and agreement, but rather by a common experience – being transformed by the Spirit of Jesus – and that alone was enough to bind them together. If we can learn anything from the example of the earliest followers of Christ, it is that unconditional commitment to community is perhaps the most important aspect of our spiritual lives. Even when we disagree or feel misunderstood, the early Christians teach us that when we value our relationships with each other more than the views we hold, we can live a life of authenticity and spiritual vibrancy.

In order to remedy my depression and loneliness, I knew I had to make a choice. Either I could continue to try to press forward on my journey alone, or I could commit to a community and live in the tension of being an unsettled wanderer within a community with which I didn't always agree. I had tried to do life on my own. That seemed like the easy option. To avoid conflict and those 'difficult conversations'. To not have accountability or direction. To be free to go wherever I wanted at any time. But none of that was healthy or worth it. If I continued to try to do this on my own, I knew my life was going to spin out of control. So, after wandering from community to community for such a long time, I decided to take a risk and commit to a church that was a tad too conservative for my taste, but which I knew was filled with people I admired and loved.

Throughout the rest of my time in college, I remained part of this community, even as my theology and social views continued to grow increasingly beyond the stated boundaries of the church. When I was eventually asked about my fluid theological views, it was done out of love and genuine concern. This community wasn't seeking to hold me back, as I thought it would, but instead it helped me to proceed with wisdom along my way. It provided me with a home I could return to in times of trial and confusion. I discovered we as a people were all at different places along the way and inevitably, someone else had had the same questions or come to the same conclusions I did. These realisations weren't earth shattering, but they provided me with a much needed reminder that I was made for community and I actually needed others to walk with me and challenge me. That's what this whole faith journey is about.

As we go about our exploring, it can be easy to think that because there is no church or group of people who see things exactly as we do that we're better off going at it alone. We may, understandably, want to avoid conflict and confusion and try to wander about tribeless. But when we disconnect from community, we miss out on the richness a diversity of perspective can bring, and find ourselves growing weary and alone. We are created for community and we must do everything in our power to establish a place and people that we can call home. Because it's only when we are in community with others that we will experience the fullness of life and step into our truest selves. It is only when we are in community that we can be sustained, challenged, and upheld, even when we end up in a ditch. We need to have others with whom we can share our doubts, pains, joys, and realisations. We all really do need somebody to lean on. Community may indeed be difficult. It's sometimes unproductive. It's always messy. But in the end, it's absolutely necessary. We need each other. That's just how we've been made.

10

Holy

*Human salvation lies in the
hands of the creatively maladjusted.*
Revd Dr Martin Luther King Jr.

When I started going to church as a young teenager, I felt like I had
to learn another language. The people at church used a language
that seemed so foreign to me. As I heard this new language
preached from the pulpit and used around me during coffee hour
after church, I did my best to go along with it and pretended I
knew what I was saying. I often heard my pastor preach about
how the many Christians in our nation were 'blaspheming' God
with their unbiblical theological and social positions. Only,
I didn't hear the word 'blaspheming', I heard 'blast-beaming'.
Every time I heard this word in church, images of liberals with
lightsabers attacking God appeared in my head. It didn't make
much sense to me, how any group of people would be able to
successfully 'blast-beam' God, but it sure sounded pretty intense.
One Sunday in youth group in the midst of a very sophisticated
theological conversation about Catholicism, I brought up how
the Catholic Church was filled with a bunch of blast-beamers
who worshipped Mary. (For any and all Catholic readers, please
accept my most sincere apology!) Immediately, the youth group

erupted in laughter. 'I think you mean "blasphemers", Brandan,' my youth pastor corrected.

I wish I could say that this was the only word in Christianese that I had publicly butchered, but it wasn't. Another strange word I heard used a lot in church was the word 'holy'. While this word was less odd to me, because I had heard it used many times throughout my life as a preface to words like 'cow' and 'crap', I still had no clue what holy actually meant. Even after many years of being a Christian, the true definition of the word was still trivial to me. Sometimes it is used to describe God in ways that make him seem far off and distant. Other times the word seems to be describing the beauty and glory of God. But if you're looking for a significant definition of the word, you're not likely to find one without doing some pretty substantial theological work. Even then, when you read what theologians write about God's holiness, they make the word seem so unreliable and incomprehensible. For most people, 'holy' is just one of those religious words that really has no substantial or particularly meaningful definition.

I have a passion for simplifying things. After getting my Bachelor's degree in Bible, Theology, and Pastoral Ministry, that passion was only intensified. I have spent many hours reading books, examining commentaries, and listening to lectures and sermons where overly educated individuals ramble on profusely about theological concepts that have been so overcomplicated the average layperson would never be able to begin to understand, or more precisely, have no good reason to try understanding. When it comes to the word 'holy', I decided to do a little digging around on my own to try to grasp what the word actually means.

When we talk about God being holy, what we're actually saying is that God is fundamentally 'different' or unique. The word denotes separateness. A one-of-a-kindness. When the Bible speaks of God as 'holy', it's always as an exclamation of just how *unique* God is compared to Creation. Make sense? Now typically, when the word holy is used, it is only in reference to God or some other sacred place or object that is 'set-apart' for service to God.

Most of us would never think of using the word 'holy' to describe any human being or ourselves. If you grew up Protestant, you probably get uncomfortable when you hear Catholics refer to the Pope as 'Holy Father' or 'His Holiness'.

But when we look to the Bible we find the most peculiar string of commands related to holiness.

> *'I am the LORD your God; consecrate yourselves and be holy, because I am holy.'*
>
> *Leviticus 11:44*

> *'Sanctify yourselves therefore, and be you holy: for I am the LORD your God.'*
>
> *Leviticus 20:7*

> *'Be holy, because I am holy.'*
>
> *1 Peter 1:16*

These are just a few references from throughout the Bible that continually call us, mere human beings, to 'be holy'. This is a command, a standard that God clearly calls us to embrace and live into. But how could we possibly 'be holy' if holiness is a characteristic unique to God? If holiness is seen as a mammoth sacred theological attribute, then there is no way humans could ever even begin to obey God's command. God might as well have said, 'Be penguins'.

But what if holiness *isn't* such a ... holy ... attribute. What if holiness was *actually* attainable? What would it look like? How would it change us? When I started exploring these questions, God began to show me a *renewed* way of understanding what it looks like to walk in step with the Spirit.

As I've already said, to be holy means to be unique or different. So when God calls us to be *holy*, we're being called to embrace our '*True Selves*,' the authentic Being God originally created us to be. Each of us has been hand crafted by the Eternal Creator of the Universe. Each of us is completely and totally unique. Truly one of a kind. From the way we look, to the way we think. Our likes and dislikes. Our inclinations. Our desires and our callings. Our giftings and our personalities. When we allow ourselves to simply *be*, to exist and express ourselves in the way God created us, beyond all of the social and cultural conditioning each of us is inevitably subjected to, we will flourish as individuals and be agents of light to the world.

Sin, like holiness, is another abstract theological term theologians spend thousands of pages musing over, trying to outline a precise definition. In Christian Theology, what separates us from God is the reality that we sin and are affected by sin. God is *holy* precisely because he is not affected by sin, like the rest of creation. But what exactly is sin? One way that sin could be defined is the participation in actions that seek to conform us to a pattern or image other than the pattern and image of God. In other words, sin is anything that tries to make us 'normal,' anything that takes away our individual uniqueness and tries to conform us to an identity other than that of our True Selves.

When the Scriptures speak about sin, they say things like 'Do not be *conformed* to the *image of this world*.' What does it mean to be 'conformed' to the 'image of this world'? It means allowing our selves to be moulded into the desires and dreams of our fallen world instead of the desires and dreams of God. When we are called to be 'like God,' we are being called to embrace our radically unique identity. Beyond all of the labels society throws on to us. Beyond all the ideals the world is seeking. God is *holy* because God is the radically *different* Creative One. To be like God is to be *different*. To be *who we truly are*, when all of the masks and false identities are stripped away. To live into the identity and dreams God has designed exclusively for us.

When we look at the few passages in the Scriptures that describe what 'heaven' or, more accurately, the *Kingdom of God* looks like, we read things like 'there is no male or female, Jew or Greek, slave or free'. We read that there is 'no marriage' and that 'all are one'. Yet at the same time, we're told people from 'every nation, tribe, and tongue' are present, in all of their diversity. The image of the Kingdom of God is one where all of the identities that currently separate us will fade into the background, while at the same time, our individual uniqueness is fully embraced and celebrated. In God's perfect world, all of the unique things that form our identity at the spiritual level remain fully intact. We're each fundamentally different from the next person. And yet, we're completely and totally united by the Spirit of God. Unity in the midst of tremendous diversity.

We begin to walk in holiness when we begin to *be ourselves*. That's what following Jesus leads to. That's the end goal of sanctification. To become fully and finally all that God intended us to be. When this happens, we don't all of a sudden become mirror images of one another. Being conformed to the image of God doesn't mean stepping in to a mould that makes us all identical. God is *far* more creative than that. The eternal and infinite Creator has an infinite number of creative ideas. No two snowflakes are identical to the other. Why would we ever assume any two humans are the same? To believe that would be to underestimate the creativity of God.

If all this is true, then Christians should be the most radically diverse group of people on the planet. But if you've hung around us for any amount of time, you'll know that this is simply not the case. Why? Because Christians love conformity. Whether it is intellectual conformity, conformity of political and social perspectives, or conformity in the way we chose to worship God. We are addicted to conformity and consensus. Usually, if someone within our community doesn't agree with our perspective or practices, we slowly begin to marginalise and push them out of our community.

But if the Kingdom of God is truly about *radical diversity* and *uniqueness,* then shouldn't the Church be about the same? What would it look like if we surrendered our addiction to uniformity and allowed for unhindered self-expression? What if we allowed room for every person's thoughts and experiences to be shared and discussed? I think we'd be pushed out of our comfort zones and be led to discover fresh insights about God and our neighbours. I think it would look a lot like heaven on earth. I think we'd begin, at last, to be the *Holy Catholic* (or universal) *Church.*

Only when we begin to realise all of our individual quirks, thoughts, desires, and expressions are truly gifts from God, given to us to enhance the world and reveal His beauty, will we begin to truly find the peace and abundance Jesus spoke so much about. To be holy is to be like Christ, and to be like Christ is to be rooted and confident in our God-given identity. No one descriptor makes up the whole of our identity – our skin colour, cultural heritage, nationality, gender expression, sexual orientation, religious affiliation, height, weight, hair colour, IQ, profession, socio-economic class, all contribute an integral part to our identity. One part doesn't make up more of us than another. These identities are each fundamental to who we are and the life God has created us to live. But when we latch on to one aspect of who we are and make it the focal point of our life, we begin to fall away from holiness. We then become more concerned about being the best Christian, the best American, the best librarian, or the best woman we can be.

Sounds noble doesn't it? Until we consider that none of us have been called to be 'the best' *anything,* other than ourselves. For me, holiness means becoming more like Brandan. I am unique and different. My expression of my cultural heritage, gender, religion, profession, sexuality, or any other aspect of my person is going to, by design, look different from yours. As it should. For me, to become more like Brandan is to become more like God, because that is in whose image I have been created. For you, seeking to be more authentically yourself, beyond the masks you've created to conceal and protect yourself and beyond all of the false identities that the world has placed on you, is what it looks like to be sanctified. To be holy.

We collectively fail to walk in holiness when we lift up an 'ideal' image as a society and seek to conform to it. When a person diverges from the normalised cultural image, we marginalise and demonise them. Those who rock the boat by being their authentic selves are often the ones society despises most. Why? Because in our bondage to our false identities, which we perceive as giving us value and security, we can't stand to see someone else walking in liberation. This is one of the reasons Jesus was so despised. As Jesus walked about the world, he embraced only his God-given identity and openly rebelled against society's moulds. He wasn't concerned about being an ideal Jew. In fact, by his society's standards, he was a *really* bad Jew. He wasn't concerned about being a 'real man' according to his patriarchal society; instead, he uplifted women and allowed them to be his disciples. He didn't try to maintain the pious identity other religious leaders worked so hard to uphold; instead, he surrounded himself with people who were considered a part of the 'wrong crowd'.

You see, Jesus' holiness was rooted in his willingness to embrace his God-given identity. That's one of the things that made him different. (Not excluding the obvious fact that he is God incarnate!) Notice, however, Jesus never denied being a Jew, a man, or a Rabbi. Of course not! Those were legitimate parts of his identity. But they weren't the *whole* of his identity. And he didn't let society tell him what each of those individual parts looked like. Jesus was *his own kind* Jew, Rabbi, and man. He was the Jew, the Rabbi, and the man God intended him to be.

What would it look like for you and me if we began to lean into God's call for us to be holy? What would it look like if we began to allow the expectations of others to fall by the wayside and instead we allowed our true colours to shine through? What if we stopped conforming to the desires others have heaped upon us year after year, and instead decided to begin working to embrace and express the person that God made us to be?

These are dangerous questions, indeed. The path towards holiness, towards conformity to the image of God, is not an easy path. But it is the only path that leads us to peace and to the abundant life God desires for us. It is the only way to live into the calling God has placed on our lives. Only when we begin to step into our True Selves, will we unlock the potential for us to fulfil the calling God has for our lives. We unleash the potential for our God-inspired dreams to become our reality. The road towards holiness is not easy. It's often marked with much pain, as we shed our false identities and rebel against the way of the world.

One of my lifelong heroes is a man you may have heard of named Martin Luther King Jr. Dr. King was a *holy* man. No, I don't mean he was perfect. But he certainly began walking on the path towards holiness. Dr. King rebelled against society's image of who he was supposed to be. As an African-American preacher, he wasn't meant to be much in the eyes of a society plagued by prejudice, but Dr. King discovered God had created him for something more. He refused to settle into the mould society had created for him. He refused to buy into the narrative that he was placed into by way of his ethnicity. He knew that only by embracing his authentic self, loving and valuing the person God had created him to be, and harnessing his God-given gifts and passions, could he live the life of greatness for which he was destined.

As Dr. King leaned into the image of God within himself, he began to ruffle some feathers. This is a common occurrence when we begin to embrace our unique selves and reject the expectations our culture places on us. Dr. King refused to be just another black preacher living under the oppressive hand of an unjust society. No, Dr. King knew he was made for more. He knew he could be a revolutionary. He knew he could change the world. He sensed God had anointed him to be a prophet for a new generation and his heart burned for justice. Many others before him had dreamed of a better day for African Americans in the United States. Many others longed for equality and liberation. Many others boldy stepped into their own holiness and paved the way for someone like Dr. King to embrace his own. But for many others still, the strong grip of oppressive conformity weighed heavily against these dreams and desires. The weight of the systemic sin of racism caused these sparks of inspiration to be quickly extinguished, and many of these would-be revolutionaries were forced to return to living within the racist status quo. But Dr. King, following the example of Jesus, dared to step out against the grain. He dared to believe he could be different. That he could be the one who actually changed the way things had been for so long. He recognised the gifts God had given him and heard the calling of God on his life. And he stepped forward in faith, embracing his true identity, rejecting the world's labels of him as a marginalised and powerless minority and standing tall as a beautiful, powerful, and one-of–a-kind son of God.

In this, Martin Luther King Jr. embraced holiness. He became something 'other,' someone unique. And through his holiness, he simultaneously inspired and infuriated many. When we embrace holiness, we go against the grain of what our culture thinks is proper. When we begin to walk in step with the Kingdom of God, we come into direct conflict with the Kingdoms of this world. Dr. King waged a mighty battle against the way of this world, but not through violence or combat. No, the weapon he used to transform the world was love. Love of himself. Love of God and God's vision for a holy world. And love of every person, just as they were, with their various quirks, experiences, and perspectives. When we begin to love the person God made us to be and begin to live into the dreams God has placed in our hearts, as crazy and unfathomable as they may be, the power of the Kingdom of God is unleashed in us and through us. Only when we find the comfort to be who we were created to be, do we become unhindered channels for the Spirit of God to flow through us and enable us to be co-creators of a better Reality for humanity.

Dr. Martin Luther King Jr. is just one example of a truly holy man. Throughout history, and indeed in each of our lives, we have encountered many holy individuals, those who live earth shattering and abundant lives that inspire us. We look at them and wonder if we could ever be like them. Could our lives really make a difference? Could our dreams really ever become our reality?

Could we truly experience the abundant life the Scriptures so often speak of? The answer is a resounding 'Yes'! And the secret to experiencing this kind of life is no secret at all. It's found clearly written in the words of Jesus, time and time again.

'Seek first the Kingdom of God and his righteousness and all of these things will be given to you' (Matthew 6:33).

Seek *first* the Kingdom. What is that Kingdom? It is that ultimate state of Reality where all of us are freed to be ourselves, to live out our dreams. This is what the Kingdom is. This is why Jesus, when asked for the location of the Kingdom of God, responds, 'The Kingdom of God is within you' (Luke 17:21). The first step of salvation, of experiencing the Reality of the Kingdom, is stepping into our true identities. When we make the bold move to be who we are, despite what society says we ought to be, we open the possibility for God to do the impossible through us. We open the door to making our dreams become reality.

This has been one of the hardest, but one of the most rewarding lessons God has taught me along my short journey of faith. When I began to trust that God didn't make a mistake with the way he created me, with all of my complexities, interests, dreams, and desires, and began to lean into my God-given identity, I began to see God do the impossible in my life. This will look different for every person, because each of us is uniquely created. But when we begin to embrace who we already are deep within, we will begin not only to experience abundant life, but we will experience a closeness and intimacy with God like never before. For we are never more like God, never more *holy*, than when we are being the individuals we were created to be. This is how we will change the world. This is salvation.

11

Fluid

*Any thing or behavior too complex to
understand becomes a phenomenon that
could be termed spiritual or magical.*

Bryant McGill

Humans are incredibly complex creations. From the $7*10^{27}$
(or seven billion billion billion) molecules that come together
to create a single human body, to the seemingly unexplainable
mysteries of consciousness and thought, the more we learn about
ourselves the more we realise what we have yet to discover. This
makes sense to me. As the only beings in the universe said to
be created in the image of the eternal Creator of the cosmos, it's
understandable that we're so complex, so mysterious. Our bodies
are made of the very stuff of the stars, the same materials that
create planets, asteroids, animals, rocks, and water. Yet, also
within each of us, there is a mysterious energy that vibrates ever
so subtly beneath the surface that gives us thoughts, emotions,
dreams, and desires. We call that indescribable yet all too familiar
field of energy the 'soul'.

With every passing generation, our understanding of ourselves
is expanded. We learn more about who we are, what we're made
of, and our place in the Universe. With every new insight we learn,

we take a baby step forward as a species. Yet at the same time, with every new breakthrough come a hundred new mysteries. This is both absolutely beautiful and incredibly frustrating as beings that are endlessly curious and profoundly convoluted. The journey into the depths of who we are is a never-ending trek, just as the journey to understand and relate to God is eternal. We are made in the image of infinity. What else should we expect?

It's interesting to me that we are able to admit the complexity of life, but then assume we've reached a place of comprehension about any single aspect of it.

This chapter is the single most difficult piece of writing I've ever felt compelled to undertake, primarily because it's about a topic that is so deeply personal I wonder if it's a wise or sane thing to attempt to write about it at all. And yet, here I am, writing about perhaps the most intimate aspect of my personhood – my sexuality. I am apprehensive to write about this, not because I have anything to be ashamed of or to hide, but rather because when someone talks about sexuality in our day and age, it often becomes the sole focus of that person's identity. My fear is that in talking about my sexuality, I will become 'Brandan, the Queer Christian'. But that's not my identity. That's not who I am. My attractions and personal relationships don't define my fundamental personhood any more than my religious affiliation or ethnicity do. Sure, sexual orientation, religion, and ethnicity all come together to make up the whole of my identity, but no single one on their own can be used to define or describe who I am. I am a Christian, but I am also so much more than a Christian. I am Scottish, but I am also so much more than a Scot, and yes, I do identify as queer, but that alone does not fundamentally define who I am as a person.

For the past year of my life, I have been involved in full-time LGBTQ activism within Christian faith communities. I stumbled into this word of being an LGBTQ activist completely by accident. For me, the trajectory was set when I was a teenager and began to discover that my sexual attractions were different. I knew I liked girls, and at the time, in fact, was in a relationship with a beautiful girl from my church. I really was attracted to her and our relationship was authentic. But at the same time, I found myself attracted to other men, at school and in church, and was terrified of what this could mean. I had often heard the pastor of my large fundamentalist Baptist church talk about this sin of 'sodomy' and knew the Bible taught homosexuality was an 'abomination'. I prayed for God to remove this sinful attraction for years, and began searching the Bible and other theological books for more clarity on the topic.

My interest in a Christian theology of sexuality and sexual ethics stayed with me through Bible college, where I was introduced to a much broader theological world of perspectives on sexuality. I continued to wrestle with my own sexual orientation and what it meant that I liked both women and men, and began to seek advice from many of the professors, pastors, and theologians who surrounded me in and around college. Every person I consulted gave me a different perspective – some recommended I pursue celibacy, others suggested that I begin reparative therapy or other healing techniques to remedy my 'sexual brokenness', and still others encouraged me to embrace these attractions as one part of who God fashioned me to be. Over the course of my time in college, I would try each of these solutions. For a period of time, I convinced myself I was going to be celibate for life. I began looking into the requirements for ordination in the Roman Catholic Church so I could be in a community that would provide accountability and a sustainable way of life for a celibate minister. This idea appealed to me for all of two months, until one day I came to my senses and realised that I could *never* live a celibate life.

Soon after, I began meeting with a professor who had found healing from his same-sex attractions through a psychological/ spiritual practice called 'Healing Prayer'. Every week for about a year, I would meet with this professor for deeply emotional and intense 'prayer sessions' where we would work through some deep-seated psychological wounds from my past that were thought to have contributed to my same-sex attractions. Over the course of the year, I experienced a lot of profound internal transformation as a result of the deep soul work that I was doing in healing prayer. Yet, despite all of the progress that helped me heal my past wounds, my attractions remained constant.

In the midst of all of these attempts to deal with and rid myself of my 'same-sex attractions', I continued to hear stories and meet people who had also walked down the same path in an attempt to find 'healing' and 'restoration' from their sexual orientation and many of their experiences were far more difficult than my own. Many of the people I began to connect with had stories of great trauma and pain. They had been forced into much more intense Christian 'therapies' that left them more deeply wounded than when they began. Many of these individuals were given the choice between celibacy or being excommunicated from their churches and families. Many walked away with so much pain and fear that they could never darken the door of a church ever again.

In this same season, I began to grow increasingly discomforted with how I was seeing the Church address LGBTQ equality on a civil level. Not only were we trying to exercise authority over the same-sex attracted people in our congregations, but we were also attempting to tell all LGBTQ people outside of our churches that they too had to adhere to our 'biblical' sexual ethics. Instead of preaching the Gospel, which invites all people to come just as they are, we began to preach a message that required LGBTQ people to conform to our standard of holiness before they were welcome into the body of Christ. Instead of working to build the Kingdom of God through subversive grassroots acts of love and justice, some Christians had chosen to address these issues in the way of the world – through power and politics. It began to become clear to me why the LGBTQ community was largely opposed to Christianity – because instead of being people that embodied the all-inclusive love of Jesus, we were a Pharisaical and hypocritical people that were doing real, tangible damage to individuals and families under the guise of 'standing for truth'.

It was because of these stories and experiences that I began to do the only thing I knew how to do to raise an issue publicly – I started to blog. My blog, *Revangelical*, existed to call for reform within Evangelicalism, and if there was any issue that needed reforming, it was this one. I wasn't sure what to do theologically with these questions surrounding same-sex attractions and relationships, and I wasn't interested in attempting to address them. They were secondary. What I *was* sure of was that Christians had failed to rightly represent the Good News of Jesus to the LGBTQ community, and we had left massive amounts of carnage in our wake. One blog post turned into five, and five into twenty, and before I knew it, I was spending a majority of my blog space talking about this issue, which made me quite popular with many at my conservative Evangelical Bible college! As I continued to wrestle through my own personal sexuality and my theology, I continued to blog about the Churches' failure to address the LGBTQ community in a Christ-like manner. And *that's* how I became an LGBTQ Christian activist.

Over time, my theological and political views around LGBTQ equality and inclusion have evolved. Through extensive study of Biblical texts that have taken me from a library in Chicago to the ruins of the ancient city of Corinth in Greece, through years of fervent prayer and listening for God, through hearing the countless stories of my LGBTQ friends, neighbours, and acquaintances, and through attempting healing and transformation of my own sexuality, I have come to change the way I view sexuality and LGBTQ issues as a person of faith. I now believe that God blesses LGBTQ marriages, that covenanted same-sex relationships are a reflection of the love and glory of God, and that identifying as both LGBTQ and Christian is not contradictory. Yet at the same time, if I am being completely honest, my beliefs about the minute details of sexuality have remained amorphous, constantly changing and evolving, taking new shapes and forms. And I think this is the way it should be. Because when we talk about sexuality, we're talking about one of the most complex aspects of our makeup as humans.

In regards to my own personal sexuality, I, like many millennials, assume the label 'queer,' which for me refers more to my entire posture of life than specifically to my sexual attractions. For me, everything is fluid. Everything changes, progresses, and evolves as we grow in experience and knowledge. Sexually, this means that I believe my attractions go both ways, but may also end up being predominately one way or the other as well. Nothing is set in stone. I feel no obligation to take on any label that would confine me to a singular sexual orientation. None of those words feel honest or authentic because my experience tells me the moment I chose to identify as straight or gay or bisexual, is the moment my feelings of attraction will change rendering that label inauthentic and inaccurate. For me, queer feels like the closest thing to a comfortable label to describe how I think about myself and how I am wired.

But my experience isn't universal. As I've already said, sexuality is complex. I hear many express their frustration because of the endless stream of new labels and language around sexual orientation and gender identity. Ten years ago, it was gay and lesbian. Then bisexual was added in. Then transgender. Then queer. Then intersex and asexual and ally. The acronym continues to grow because as we enter into an age where conversations around sexual orientation and gender identity are becoming less taboo, more people are being freed to be honest and to discuss their unique internal wiring. These orientations aren't new. However, discussing them openly is becoming more common now that public shame around these topics is dissipating. For as many unique people as there are, there are that many sexual orientations, gender identities, personalities, spiritualities, and psychologies. As we enter into a period in human history where we are finally discovering the infinite creativity of the Universe and the intrinsic uniqueness of every molecule and atom, we will continue to be blown away by the eccentricity of every person.

Fluid

We're all fluid. We all change and morph. We are always progressing. We will always grow. This is part of what it means to be created in the image and likeness of an infinite and expansive God. The sooner we relinquish our desire to label and classify each other in neat boxes where we can understand and ultimately control each other, the sooner we open up ourselves and our world to true freedom. In that realm of freedom, where we are liberated to simply be the person we have been uniquely crafted to be by God, our focus shifts away from the question of *who* we love to *how* we love. We begin to understand that sexuality, like any other aspect of our personhood, is morally neutral, and the choices we make as fully integrated individuals are where the real questions of justice and morality lie.

Whenever there is change or progress, there is also usually fear. We fear every time there is a shift in our world because we have become accustomed to and comfortable with things the way they are. Whenever something new is discovered that changes the way we view our lives and our world, we always respond with apprehension and resistance. We're living in an amazing period of enlightenment with regard to human sexuality, and all of us, to some degree or another, have been apprehensive. This apprehension manifests itself in very different ways. For some, it manifests as violent resistance to change. For others, it appears as deep anxiety. For others still, it manifests as a guarded curiosity. For me, I still struggle with accepting the fluidity of my sexual orientation. I struggle with the wide array of questions and fears that come with the dissolving of the old way of understanding the sexual and psychological makeup of humans. But the more I have allowed my fears to fade to the backdrop as I have opened my heart and mind to the possibility that things are not always as clean as we once thought, I have tasted a liberation and beauty words cannot begin to describe. For there is nothing more magnificent than giving ourselves freedom to be who we really are without fear of condemnation or judgement. I know I haven't even begun to understand the complex creation that is me, but with every new step we take as a people, I have decided to try to remain open. The jury isn't out on us yet. No book, no religion, no field of science has even come close to explaining who we are, and I suspect they never will.

This may seem like a peculiar way to end a chapter on sexuality. But I've discovered these conversations are only tangentially about sexuality. They're also much bigger than attractions and orientations. They're about the fundamental ways we view the world. They're about how we interact with knowledge and progress. They're about how we see ourselves as people in the world. They're questions about why we are here and where we are heading. In all of this, we can be sure of only one thing: our world is expanding. Our understanding is growing. Things aren't becoming simpler, they're becoming much more complex and diverse. The more we go deeper and wider into our quest to probe the depths of reality, the less our categories and understanding of the world become relevant. As we continue to turn over each new stone and unravel our conception of what it means to be human, may we abandon fear, release our apprehension, and allow the River of Life to propel us forward, closer and closer into that great, expansive Ocean we know as God. The river may be turbulent at times, but if we surrender our doubts, and trust that the Force that guides us is good and is pulling us towards freedom, then we may release ourselves to the mighty current and enter into to the fullness of Life.

12

Eucharist

Christ, my life, possess me utterly.
Take and make a little Christ of me.

George MacDonald

If you grew up in a Baptist church like I did, then you know that Baptists like to eat. Any and every time there is an occasion worth celebrating, a good Baptist church will call for a time of 'fellowship'.

All of the Baptists moms would go home to their kitchens and begin whipping up one of their favourite recipes, usually something quite unhealthy, but tasty. The morning of the 'fellowship' an endless stream of women would head downstairs with their foil-covered dishes, filling the church building with a variety of delectable scents. Throughout the entire church service, everyone sits on the edge of their pew as their stomachs grumble, waiting to sing that last hymn so that we can all go downstairs and *finally* get to eating. Once everyone is downstairs and has filled their plates with all of the food they could eat and still feel like they weren't sinning, the roar of laughter and conversation would fill the room. Hour after hour, church folks would sit around talking about everything and anything, genuinely enjoying the company of their friends. These times of fellowship are some of the sweetest memories I have from back in my Baptist days.

Food and eating have long been seen as tools for encouraging people to bond with each other. Since ancient times, sitting down and having a meal with friends and strangers has been seen as the primary way that we can build relationship with one another. The whole concept of cooking something for each other, bringing it to the table to share, and enjoying the company of one another as you feast on the wide array of dishes has a way of disarming everyone at the table and allowing true fellowship to flow. It makes sense, then, that one of the earliest Christian rituals was a feast. Throughout Church history, this feast has come to be known by many different names. Some call it 'The Lord's Supper', others 'Communion', still others 'The Agape Feast', but the name that is most commonly used to refer to this meal is 'The Eucharist'. When this ritual was established by Jesus on the night of his betrayal and arrest, he told his disciples that every time they gathered for a meal, they should take bread and wine, break it and share it, 'in memory of him'. Why did Jesus view this ritual as so essential? Why do we still practice it to this day?

Growing up as an Evangelical, I never really got what the whole communion thing was all about. I knew that it was commanded in Scripture, so I understood why we did it. But for me, it was never particularly meaningful. Whenever I would take the elements – a tiny piece of Wonderbread and a sip of grape juice – I would picture Jesus dying on the cross and ask God to forgive me of my sins. Then, I'd eat the bread, drink the juice, and we would move on. It all seemed rather trivial. I knew that other Christians, like the Catholics, viewed this ritual as essential to worship, performing it every single service, instead of once a month like my church did. But I didn't understand why. What could be so important about this? Why did eating this sacred snack together have such a prominent place in the New Testament? What was Jesus really getting at? It wasn't until I began to explore the ancient traditions of the Church that the importance of the Eucharist began to radically change the way I viewed Christianity altogether.

The earliest Christians were a people of rhythms. They used rituals and other fixed practices to help ground them in the faith and constantly remind them of the way of Jesus. The practice of the Eucharist became an essential part of the life of all disciples of Jesus from the very beginning because in it, two vital truths were communicated. The first was that at the Table of the Lord where the Eucharist was served, all people are equal. Women and men. Gentile and Jewish. Rich and poor. Sick and healthy. Old and young. When we gather at God's table, we gather as one people, one body, united by the sacrifice of Jesus at the cross. We gather as one people, unified in the midst of our abundant diversity by our common allegiance to our one faith, one hope, and one Lord. The Eucharist was the great equaliser. For one moment of time, all of us stood on level ground. All our prejudices and biases were forced to fade into the background. We came together as one broken but connected body in need of grace.

The Eucharist also reminded early believers of a second truth - the pattern of life that they were to live. When Christ commanded us to do this ritual 'to remember and proclaim his death until he comes again', he was asking us to remember the way of life that he lived and to follow him in it. The cross of Christ served not only as the atonement for the sins of humanity, but also as the way in which all people should live their lives. On the cross, Jesus allowed his body to be broken open and his blood to be shed for the healing of the world. Through his gracious self-sacrifice, redemption and restoration became possible for the world. In the Eucharist, through the breaking of bread and the pouring of wine, we are reminded of Jesus' sacrifice for our salvation. By participating in the Eucharist, eating the bread and drinking the wine, disciples unite themselves to the mission of God in Christ. We become one in Christ and one with Christ's radical mission of redemption. At the Eucharist, Christians are reminded that the pattern by which we are to live is one of breaking ourselves open and pouring ourselves out for the redemption of the world. In other words, the Eucharist reminds us to live our lives as ministers of reconciliation, as living sacrifices, as members of the Body of Christ. The Eucharist reminds us of the mystery that the Spirit of God indwells us and has truly made us the hands and feet of Jesus to our world.

The reason that the Eucharist has held such a primary place in the life of the Church throughout the ages is because it is the singular place where we can come to receive grace, be united with God, and be sent out into the world as God's agents of redemption. The Eucharist provides a place for us to come with all of our baggage, drop it off, and be filled again with the Bread of Life and the Cup of Salvation. When we come away from the table each week, we can be confident of our standing before God. We can be confident that Christ's life resides within us. That we have been made one with God and have been commissioned to be his power, person, and presence to our community, culture, and world. How many of us actually believe that? That we have been *so* filled with God's Spirit, that we are truly *one* with Christ, agents of his redemptive work in the world? That we are co-conspirators with God in the renewal of all things. In the consummation of the Kingdom of God on earth as it is in heaven?

This radical notion of union with Christ has been lost in the Western Church today. We have forgotten what it looks like to be a true disciple of Jesus. Perhaps, it's because we have generally decentralised the place of the Eucharist in our Spiritual lives. Western Christianity has forgotten the truth of the incarnation, that God put on flesh in the person of Jesus and continues to re-incarnate himself in the hearts of his children. Instead, our faith has become increasingly gnostic, relying on knowledge *about* God instead of participation *in God* to be our salvation. When our faith becomes more about knowledge of God than about living as the presence of God to our world, we inevitably will shift away from crucial aspects of what it means to be a disciple of Christ, such as feeding the poor, healing the sick, setting the oppressed free, uplifting the marginalised, and the other justice-oriented aspects of Jesus' life and teaching. When our faith is more focused on knowing theology about God instead of a deep, mystical union with God, demonstrated through the ritual of the Eucharist, we ultimately wander off the path of true discipleship. The Eucharist is more than just a sacrament or a ritual. For Christians, it is a way of life. It is to be for us a constant reminder of our call to break ourselves open and pour ourselves out for the healing and redemption of the world. It is a practice that centres us on Jesus and his radical way of justice, it helps us to seek first the Kingdom of God and his righteous reign.

Since the earliest days of our faith, to be a Christian was to be committed to justice for all people. Yet, in recent times, many denominations of Christianity have moved to a place of intense opposition to such a teaching. Throughout most of my life of faith, I was fearful of any preacher who would preach about the importance of doing 'justice'. In fact, I remember watching the *Glenn Beck Show* as a teenager and hearing Glenn urge conservative Christians to immediately leave any church whose preacher used the words 'social justice' from the pulpit. These ideas of activism and justice were seen as liberal perversions of the Gospel. For some, the idea that doing acts of justice was a requirement of Christians seemed like a shift away from the Reformed teachings of salvation by grace alone, through faith alone, apart from works. For others, the opposition to social justice teachings was a reactionary position arising out of, yet again, the Fundamentalist/Modernist controversy of the early twentieth century. As 'liberals' embraced science and began doubting the supernatural, a new emphasis was placed on the moral teachings of Christ. For some, the Gospel became not about supernatural salvation from sin or hell, but about building a better world through tangible acts of justice. This emphasis away from understanding Christ in supernatural terms and rendering him as nothing more than a moral teacher was seen as a supreme heresy by those who began identifying as 'Fundamentalists'.

Decades since the climax of this controversy, many Christians are still fearful of 'social justice' language. Much of the teaching coming from Evangelical pulpits today still places the primary emphasis on saving the souls of our world rather than feeding the hungry or caring for the environment. Dr Al Mohler, the President of Southern Seminary, the largest Evangelical seminary in the world, wrote concerning social justice:

> *'The church's main message must be [the] Gospel. The New Testament is stunningly silent on any plan for governmental or social action. The apostles launched no social reform movement. Instead, they preached the Gospel of Christ and planted Gospel churches.'[1]*

This sort of harsh reaction against any understanding of the Gospel that includes social action at its core is commonplace in many Christian communities today. But when we, through the Eucharist, are called back to the very heart of the Gospel, we see a radically different message. The cross of Jesus did, in fact, accomplish cosmic salvation for the world. On the cross, Jesus did atone for the sins of humanity. And that *is* good news. But it's not *the whole* news. The cross simultaneously shows us the salvific love of God for humanity, while at the same time, calls us to go and do likewise. The cross is not only the place where we are to come to find forgiveness of our sins, but it is also the place where we go to understand how we are to live as disciples. If our Rabbi laid down his life for the redemption of the world, then we too must follow in his footsteps. And when Christians throughout the centuries came to the Lord's Table to partake of the Eucharist, this is what they were reminded of. There, they received anew the grace and mercy of God. There they also were reminded of their union with Christ, filled with his body and blood, and sent to

---

1 Dr. Albert Mohler, *Glenn Beck, Social Justice, and the Limits of Public Discourse*, http://www.albertmohler.com/2010/03/15/glenn-beck-social-justice-and-the-limits-of-public-discourse/

pour themselves out for the redemption of the world. This is what it means to be a disciple, a devotee, a follower of Jesus.

As I wrestled through these questions, I once again found myself drawn to the Scriptures to seek guidance. If I wanted to know what it meant to be a follower of Jesus, it made sense to take some time to study what Jesus himself said. So, I opened up to the Gospel of Matthew and began to listen to the words of Jesus every day for a few months.

To my surprise, Jesus didn't help me out one bit. At least not in the way I expected him to. Instead of solidifying the beliefs about what it looked like to be a Christian, Jesus only seemed to wear away the remaining presuppositions I had. When I read the words of Jesus, I found a message that was radically different from everything that I had come to believe to be true. Instead of focusing on right beliefs, Jesus called his disciples to live lives of radical justice and mercy to their friends, neighbours, and even enemies. In fact, it seemed that the people Jesus spent most of his time preaching against were those who held theological certainty as their highest value instead of engaging in social justice. As I read Jesus words, I heard him speaking to me. I was the Pharisee. I had wrapped my whole faith in having the 'right' theology. I believed that those who put doing tangible acts of justice over teaching theology and preaching the Bible were going liberal and had abandoned the Gospel. But when I took time to focus on the words of Jesus, I began to discover just the opposite was true.

The Pharisees and teachers of the Law had the Torah down pat. They were rooted in the Bible. They advocated for right belief and adherence to Scriptural principles among the Jewish people. To me, they seemed to be excellent Christians. Yet, when Christ himself shows up on the scene and says: *'Woe to you, scribes and Pharisees! For you lock people out of the kingdom of heaven. For you do not go in yourselves, and when others are going in, you stop them. You cross sea and land to make a single convert, and you make the new convert twice as much a child of hell as yourselves!'* (Matthew 23:13-15) and *'Woe to you, scribes and Pharisees! For you tithe mint, dill, and cumin, and have neglected the weightier matters of the law: justice and mercy and faith!'* (Matthew 23:23) When Jesus speaks of salvation, he talks of it in terms of those who do justice and not in terms of those who have the correct theology and doctrine. Jesus seemed less concerned about whether his disciples were exemplary theologians and more concerned with whether or not they embodied grace, forgiveness, and peace to their neighbours, their enemies, and themselves.

Day after day, as I read through the Gospels, I found myself arguing with Jesus. Frankly, he seemed to have pretty watered-down faith. In fact, based on my understanding of what it meant to be a Christian, I don't think Jesus would even come close to hitting the mark. As I began to think about the implications of that realisation, I began to really wonder if perhaps I had believed a very faulty understanding of the Christian faith. There was obviously something very wrong with my understanding of Christianity if Jesus himself wouldn't be a part of it. It seemed to me that if I wanted to discover what exactly true Christianity was, I would have to start from scratch, beginning with Jesus' teachings in the Gospels and work my way up from there. And as I began reformulating my faith based on Jesus, everything became more and more uncomfortable.

According to the Gospels, Jesus is the word of God made flesh. God Almighty stepping out of his heavenly abode, putting on flesh and blood, and entering into Creation. Or as Eugene Peterson puts it in *The Message*, God 'moved into the neighbourhood' (John 1:14 MSG). When God chose to become incarnate, he didn't choose to be born in a palace of gold as the child of royalty. No, when God chose to come to earth, he came in the form of a peasant – a child born into the most undignified circumstances. The incarnation of God is the first and highest of all *sacraments* – or 'sacred mysteries'. In it, God demonstrates to humanity how we ought to live. Being willing to step out of our places of comfort, privilege, and power, into undignified and uncomfortable circumstances. Being willing to lose our lives for the sake of gaining eternal life. Being willing to give it all away in order to gain the Kingdom. These are the mysteries that comprise the heart of Christ's message. And by the time we arrive at the end of the Gospel narrative, we find Christ instituting the ritual we have come to know as the *Eucharist*.

But more than anything, the Eucharist, like the incarnation, is meant to be a pattern of life in which we live. One of the reasons the early Christians were so adamant about partaking of the Eucharist is because it reminded them of the rhythm that they were supposed to be in step with as they lived their lives. The pattern of breaking open our bodies and pouring out our lives for the redemption and healing of the world. Is this not the example that Christ left for us? Is this not what Christ has called us to do? When we gather at the communion table, all of our other identities fall to the background. We come as one body, the Body of Christ, God's incarnations on earth as in heaven. When we partake of the elements of bread and wine, we are mysteriously united to Christ, filled and nourished, ready to be sent out into the world to break our own bodies open and pour our selves out to the poor, the oppressed, the sinful, and the marginalised. The Eucharist reminds us that Christ's sacrifice is for all people and that we have been commissioned to take that sacrifice – in message and in deed – to the world. We come to the table to be recalibrated, reminded, and rejuvenated so that we may go to the ends of the earth as ambassadors and incarnations of Jesus.

The ritual of the Eucharist provides the image of what it looks like to be a Christian. Beyond having the right answers or believing the right things about God, being a Christian is first and foremost about following Christ. About being filled with the Spirit of God, and allowing ourselves to be broken and poured out in the world. The Eucharistic life beckons us to do justice and to sacrifice ourselves. When we begin to view the life of disciples of Christ through the lens of the Eucharist, many other teachings throughout the New Testament become clear. For instance, when the Apostle Paul tells us to '*to offer [our] bodies as a living sacrifice, holy and pleasing to God--this is [our] true and proper worship'* (Romans 12:1 NIV), he is directly paralleling the example of Christ as demonstrated through the Eucharist. This command isn't simply instructing us to be pure and pious. Instead, it is a command to do justice. Paul parallels the words of the Prophets Isaiah and Micah who describe 'true and proper worship' as *'Free the people you have put in prison unfairly and undo their chains. Free those to whom you are unfair and stop their hard labour. Share your food with the hungry and bring poor, homeless people into your own homes. When you see someone who has no clothes, give him yours, and don't refuse to help your own relatives.'* (Isaiah 58:6-7 NCV) Also, *'You say, "What can I bring with me when I come before the Lord, when I bow before God on high?"....The Lord has told you, human, what is good; he has told you what he wants from you: to do what is right to other people, love being kind to others, and live humbly, obeying your God.'* (Micah 6:6-8 NCV) The pleasing sacrifice that Paul is speaking of is the sacrifice of our lives in service of one another. The only worship and fasting God desires from us is to give of ourselves to heal the world. This is what Jesus did his entire life. This is what Jesus did in his death. And this is what Jesus continues to do through the hands and feet of his disciples around the world.

To be a Christian is to live a Eucharistic life. It is to come to the table where we are all equal, brothers and sisters made in the image and likeness of God. It is to recognise and live into our status as children of God, united with Christ, and transformed into his body on the earth. It is also to live in such a way that we are constantly giving of ourselves to the world. Pouring out our lives for the poor, marginalised, and oppressed. To live a Eucharistic life is to live a life centred on Jesus and his Gospel. To live a life where we seek the expansion of the Kingdom of God through one subversive act of love at a time. We have been called to be the power, person, and presence of Christ to our world. This is what we are reminded of when we come to the table together.

13

Grace

Grace isn't about having a second chance;
grace is having so many chances that you could use them
through all eternity and never come up empty.
Shauna Niequist

Grace. What a word. In Christian circles, the word grace is tossed
around in thousands of different ways. Sometimes it's referring to
God's forgiveness displayed through the death and resurrection of
Jesus. Sometimes it's referring to an abstract theological principle
that is supposedly at the core of what it means to be a Christian.
Other times, grace refers to something that is beautiful or skillful;
a dancer or a painter can be said to be full of grace. But for me,
grace isn't an abstract theological concept or a frivolous adjective.
It's a way of life.

The fact that I am still standing today, full of faith and hope for
the future (most of the time anyway) - that is grace. The friends
and mentors that God has brought along my path, who have
sojourned with me and offered me guidance in my meanderings -
that is grace. The valuable life lessons that I have learned in every
church and spiritual community that I have been a part of - that is
grace. Grace is a very real, tangible experience that lies at the very
heart of what it means to be reconciled to God and also to be a

minister of reconciliation. It's the space that we give ourselves and others to stumble and fall without judgement or condemnation. It's the hand we extend to help lift up those who have wronged us when they have fallen. Grace is the one thing that can heal all our wounds, bridge all of our divides, and ultimately save all of our souls. Grace *alone*.

Grace is as hard to live out as it is to experience. It's a radical notion that flips upside down every part of our lives. Grace, when properly understood, calls us out from comfort and in to some of the most painful situations and circumstances for the sake of bringing healing and redemption to our world.

After I became a Christian, I still found myself living in a very toxic and dysfunctional environment. Coming to Jesus didn't magically change the circumstances of my life. Though I had found redemption, I still had to return to my life that was clouded by the darkness of sin. Each afternoon, I would walk up the street from the bus stop to my house, checking to see if my dad was stumbling around drunk outside or if he had wandered off to a neighbour's trailer. If he wasn't home, I'd hurry inside and lock the door, keeping him from coming in and harassing me all afternoon. If he was home, I would try to make it inside without acknowledging him, lock myself in my room, turn on the Christian television networks, and ignore his repeated attempts to mess with me. Inevitably, however, the day would end with a fight. Whether between my dad and me or between my mom and dad, if my dad was drinking, there was going to be an argument that would eventually escalate into full-scale war. Night after night, I found myself on my knees in my room, eyes swollen and red from all the tears, begging God to take me out of these circumstances. I couldn't understand why God would allow me and my family to go through so much pain.

In the midst of my pain and suffering, God began to teach me the truth about grace. The lesson would take me years to begin to realise, but once I began to get a grasp of the power of grace, my eyes were opened and I began to see my life and my suffering with a new set of lenses.

All the way through High School, I resented my father for the abuse that he subjected me to. Before I left for college, I had made sure that my father was finally arrested in order to end my mom's suffering when I moved to Chicago. After my dad was put in prison for his abuse, my mom moved out of our trailer and to another town. I knew that my dad would have a hard time finding her when he was finally out of prison. When I left home for college, I never intended to see or hear from my father again. And that was absolutely fine by me.

Over the course of my first semester, I was forced to begin dealing with a lot of my internal junk that had accumulated throughout my childhood. Now that I was living thousands of miles away from home 'on my own', I was faced with the reality that I was becoming an adult. Life was going to look fundamentally different. I realised that that I had made it through my childhood, that I was finally free from abuse. But I also recognised that severe damage had been done to my soul. The anger and malice I had bottled up for nearly two decades finally began to be released in the form of a deep depression and severe panic attacks. My freshman year was filled with late nights weeping in the utility closet on my dormitory floor. I would wake in the middle of the night in deep panic, feeling like I was going to die. One night, the attack became so severe that my RA ended up calling an ambulance and having me taken to the emergency room.

Earlier that day I had been on the phone with my mom. She told me that my dad had been released from prison and that he had been living on the streets. I wasn't sure how she knew this information, but it didn't bother me much. My mom continued to tell me that my dad had attempted to hurt himself and called her from the hospital earlier in the week. I felt my body begin to tense up. She then said the very thing I was most afraid of. She told me that she had gone to visit him in the hospital and that he was now back living with her. She assured me that he had changed. That he was no longer drinking. That he was on a new path. My face turned red with anger and my body grew weak. I think I swore and then hung up the phone. A wave of emotions swept over me. Anger at my mom for allowing my father to come back into our lives. Sadness and confusion over the fact that my dad had tried to harm himself. Fear of what would happen when I returned home for Christmas in just a few weeks. The rest of that day became a blur, until I woke up late that evening in sheer panic.

After spending the night in the hospital, I knew that something had to change. I knew that my anxiety was a result both of mental damage that had been done throughout my childhood and a profound fear. I feared what life would look like now that my mom and dad were back together. I also feared what would happen if my dad truly did turn his life around. I felt a little like I imagine the Prophet Jonah must have felt when God told him that he planned to save the Ninehvites. I had spent eighteen years under the abuse and dysfunction of this man. Now, after six months away, he's all of a sudden 'changed'? I doubted that it was true. But more than that, I didn't want it to be true. I wanted more time to feel bad for myself. I wanted to have someone to blame for the struggles I faced. I wanted to have an excuse to continue justifying my own dysfunction.

As the time approached for me to return home for Christmas and be reunited with my father for the first time in over a year, I spent a lot of time in prayer. I asked God to heal my heart. To help me to love like He loves. Over time as I prayed, a word came to the surface of my mind. That word was *grace*. At the time, grace was more of a theological concept for me than it was anything practical. I wasn't sure what to do with 'grace' or why it kept resurfacing in my times of prayer. In order to find more direction, I looked to the pages of Scripture to read about grace. And inevitably, as I read, I was led to the clearest demonstration of grace ever to happen – the cross.

No matter what you may believe actually took place when Rabbi Jesus was crucified, we can all agree with great confidence that the events of Good Friday forever changed the course of human history. Jesus' death was the very epitome of injustice. He had committed no crime. He had done no one any harm. However, his message about the Kingdom of God and his lax attitude when it came to upholding the religious laws of the Jews had offended the Roman government and the Jewish religious leaders respectively. As Jesus' message gained a following, they feared that he would gain power and inevitably overthrow their rule. We know, however, that this was not Jesus' goal at all. None the less, the religious leaders and government officials conspired together to kill Jesus. Throughout his arrest, his trial, his torture, and his crucifixion, the attitude that Jesus kept was one of pure, undiluted grace. As the government officials mocked him and beat him, he did not retaliate with anger or utter an unkind word. As they flogged him, spat on him, and hung him high upon a cross, he looked down and didn't speak a single word of curse. Instead, he pronounced forgiveness. 'Father, forgive them, for they don't know what they are doing.' (Luke 23:34) At the worst point of his suffering, Christ demonstrated the power of grace. In the midst of his pain, in the midst of insults and curses being hurled, in the midst of his humiliation, he didn't play into the hands of injustice. He didn't return a curse for a curse. He didn't call on his disciples to fight those who were murdering him. Instead, he looks down into his murderers' eyes and utters a word of forgiveness. That is grace.

Jesus' demonstration of grace spoke clearly to my situation: I needed to demonstrate grace to my father, who had harmed me. Only in extending forgiveness and blessing to him could the power of resentment and pain be broken in my life. Grace not only would be the key to healing my own soul, but it had the potential to unlock healing in my dad's life as well. I didn't know what extending grace would look like for me when I returned home, but I was determined to give it to my dad, no matter what my experience with him was like.

When my flight from Chicago landed home in Baltimore just a few days before Christmas, I walked off the jet bridge more slowly than usual. I knew that in just a few moments, I would be reunited with my mom and dad who had come to pick me up from the airport. My heart pounded in my chest. I wanted more than anything to get back on the plane, rather than have to face whatever lay before me. But I continued, slowly, towards the baggage claim area, whispering fervent prayers under my breath with every step. As I turned the corner to exit the secured area, I saw my mom standing tall with a bright smile and arms extended to welcome me home. Next to her stood a man I barely recognised. Skinnier than normal, shaved head, frail looking. It was my father. He stood awkwardly to the side of my mom and I as we hugged, not saying a word. I stepped over towards him and extended my arms giving him a quick hug. In that moment, tears welled up in both of our eyes. Though no words were spoken, there was a palpable sense of release.

Just a few weeks before, I had expected never to see my dad again, and I was okay with that. Bitterness and pain clouded my thinking. But now, in a moment, my heart was softened. And I sensed that my dad's was too. We walked to my mom's car quietly, not saying a word to each other. Yet, there was a sense that everything was going to be okay. The next couple of weeks were quite awkward and uncomfortable. My dad and I felt like we had to get to know each other all over again. We spent many days having short conversations with one another when my mom was at work. It was hard for me to talk to him and clearly for him to talk to me. But we did it. I worked hard to try to extend blessings to him. I prayed for him regularly. I bought him gifts at Christmas, a small sign of forgiveness. By the end of my three-week winter vacation, there was a real sense that reconciliation had begun. I had also learned just how hard and just how powerful grace can be. A few weeks of kindness instead of resentment opened the door for healing and restoration of 18 years' worth of pain. Over the next semester, I would spend time talking to my dad on the phone from Chicago, intentionally showing him that I was working on forgiveness. I began going to counselling to work through my own pain. And I continued to try to demonstrate the grace that God had extended to me through Jesus.

Throughout life, we will inevitably experience a lot of pain at the hands of other people. We are broken. We will hurt each other. We all have been wounded. And the way that many of us respond to such situations is by hurting other people. With my dad, the easiest and most satisfying response would have been to refuse to speak to him or to call up all of his past mistakes. My natural impulse is to want to defend myself and to retaliate. 'An eye for an eye' as Moses wrote in the Book of Leviticus. How satisfying to cause harm to those who have harmed us! The problem is that when we treat others the way they have treated us, we only further injustice. When we refuse to forgive our oppressor we will only add more fuel to the fire of oppression. If I had retaliated against my father, he might possibly have have returned to drinking, or worse. He might have fallen deeper into the cycle of addiction and abuse. But the way of grace calls us to extend *favour* to the least deserving of people. It calls us to *bless* those who constantly curse us. It calls for us to *love* those who spew hatred at us. It calls us to *lift up* the very person or people who constantly tear us down. It is radically counterintuitive. It seems foolish, unwise, and unrealistic. We can come up with a million rational excuses for why being gracious is not the best course of action. Won'twe be just encouraging their sinful behaviour? Won't we only give more power to their unjust attitudes? In order to answer these questions, we need only look back at the cross.

My situation with my dad is only one small example of the power of grace. I don't tell it to demonstrate my own spiritual maturity, but rather how God's grace can work in the midst of some of the most spiritually stunted and injured individuals. Many of us have been severely hurt by people in our lives. Many have faced abuse from family members and spiritual leaders that is incomparable to what I've described in these pages. I have heard stories from many of my LGBTQ friends who have been humiliated by church leaders and rejected by their faith communities. I have sat with people who have been mocked and ridiculed by their friends and family for expressing their questions and doubts. In every situation where there has been hurt or offence, there is also still hope for healing and restoration. When we think back to unjust situations in our past, the last thing we might want to do is extend grace. I certainly didn't want to. To the natural mind, it seems absurd to assert that the way to foster healing from a toxic or abusive situation is to return to the situation and offer forgiveness, blessing, and love. But this is the way of the Kingdom. This is the way of true inner healing. When we are able to genuinely speak words of forgiveness and blessing into the pains and injustices we have faced, we prevent the abuse from having any further power over our lives and at the same time liberate the abuser of shame and guilt. Our natural impulse may be to disconnect from the toxic environment, such as a church community or family, altogether. To cut off all relationship and communication with the ones who have offended us. And in some extreme situations, where our physical and mental wellbeing may be in jeopardy, this may indeed be a necessary course of action. But whenever we have the opportunity, we should seek to allow grace to flow through us. Not only will it bring healing to our own souls, but it has the potential to completely redeem a situation, a person, and even a community.

The more I have experienced the power of grace over the last few years, the more I have looked for opportunities to be a channel for grace to enter in and redeem some of the worst situations. For instance, in the fundamentalist church I have talked so much about in this book. While it's clear I still have some wounds to be healed, a few years back, God really convicted my heart about forgiving and reconciling with the community where I had experienced rejection and marginalisation. During that period, I sent emails and called the pastor numerous times in an attempt to ask for forgiveness of any wrongdoing on my part and to bless the church and the ministry that had led me to faith to begin with. After many weeks of effort, I received no response. Initially I was very disheartened. 'Of course, they would ignore my attempts to be gracious!' I thought.

But in the midst of this internal conflict, I was reminded that even if my old pastor *never spoke to me again*, I could still extend grace. I could still speak blessings instead of curses over the community. One day, after trying to call the pastor's office a final time with no luck, I set down my phone and prayed. I asked God to bless the church and all who attended. I thanked God for the role that the community and the pastor played in my life and faith formation. I prayed for them to become a community where grace continued to flow to the entire world. After I prayed, I clicked on to the church's website and began listening to a recent sermon from my old pastor. As I listened, a sense of joy sprung up within my soul. Tears began to flow down my face. But this time, they weren't tears from pain. They were tears of peace. Of joy. For the first time in nearly six years, I was able to listen to a sermon by this pastor and not shut down in pain and anxiety. No, I had moved to a place where, whether he ever received it or not, I had forgiven him. Not just that. I had blessed him. I truly wished for his best. I truly wanted to see the ministry of the church to prosper. It seemed absolutely crazy. But I realised, in this moment, I had moved on. I had been freed from the bitterness of my past. This didn't mean that I was going to stop raising my voice about the injustices I experienced within a fundamentalist community. This didn't mean I was condoning the wrong that was done to me. But what it did mean was that I was no longer captive to it. That when I spoke of it, I spoke out of a place of genuine warmth towards this church, caring deeply for them and hoping for real change to take place in their midst. I spoke not as an enemy of the church, but as an ally. Not as a critic, but as an advocate. This is the difference that grace makes.

When I think back to Jesus' example of grace, demonstrated not only at the cross, but throughout his entire life, I am still astounded. Jesus was not a fluffy hippie who just ignored injustice in favour of 'peace'. No, he was actively involved in calling out injustice and speaking truth to power. He called sinners to repentance. He confronted evil head on. And at the same time, he lifted up sinners. He offered healing and extended forgiveness to those who despised him. He shared a meal with his so-called friend who he knew would soon betray him. He spoke with respect to the officials who unjustly tried him. And from the cross, the place of supreme injustice, he declared a word of grace. To his murderers. To his followers. To the world. And in that moment, he showed how grace completely destroys the forces of evil and injustice. Grace strips sin of its power and heals the offender and the offended. In our lives, we are called to extend this kind of grace. Radical, unconditional, messy grace. We are called to return to the people and places that have done us wrong and to extend our arms to embrace them. This is the only way that healing can begin. This is the only way that injustice can be overturned. This is how God has redeemed every one of us. And this is how we must redeem each other.

The way of grace isn't the easiest path. It doesn't make the past go away. But what it does do is offer a new beginning for everyone involved. With my dad, I was freed from living my life in response to his neglect and abuse. He was freed from the burden of guilt and shame. Today, things may not be perfect, but healing has begun. Grace has reunited a son to a father he never thought he'd see again. Grace has taught me to love and value the church that brought me to faith, even in the midst of all the wrong that was done. And time and time again, grace has covered my failures, healed my wounds, and liberated me from slavery to shame. Grace.

14

Journey

Life is a journey.
When we stop,
things don't go right.

Pope Francis

One of my favourite stories in the entire Bible is the story of the call of Abram in Genesis 12. From the earliest days of my faith, I have consistently been compelled by the character of Abram and his journey towards becoming arguably the most significant spiritual leader in human history. We meet Abram for the first time in Genesis 12, where he seemingly appears out of nowhere. We're told that one day Abram was walking along when he suddenly hears the voice of God speaking to him.

'Abram, leave everything you own, your inheritance, your land, and your family and depart for a land that I will show you. If you do, I will bless you abundantly and make you the father of many nations.'

I have often wondered what it must have been like for Abram to receive such a direct but seemingly random command telling him to leave everything his family had worked to build for generations and start walking to God knows where (but literally!). If I was Abram, I'd want to take some time to consider the circumstances. Was that voice really God? Or am I just dehydrated from walking out here in the desert too long? If it is God, he's going to have to give me some more detailed directions than 'start walking'. I'd probably want to talk over the situation with my wife and family, maybe spend some time praying about it. I mean, talk about a radical change of life.

But, according to the biblical text, Abram does no such thing. He asks no such questions. Instead, we read in verse 4 of Genesis 12, 'So Abram departed ...' He heard the voice of God and the next thing we're told is that Abram departed. He left. He went home, packed his bags, loaded up his donkey, summoned his wife, and left. Not having the slightest idea where he was going, why he was going there, or how God's grandiose promises could even possibly be fulfilled. But he moved forward, trusting that what he had experienced was truly God and that this God would be faithful to guide him, lead him, and provide everything he would need. It's this kind of radical faith that earned Abram the reputation he has throughout not only the rest of the Scriptures, but as the father of the three most prominent religions in the world: Judaism, Christianity, and Islam, also known as 'the Abrahamic faiths'.

One reason that I really resonate with the story of Abram's calling is because it is very archetypal of my own personal journey of faith. When I embarked on my journey towards the 'promised land' at the age of twelve, I had no clue what I was doing or where I was going. All that I really knew was that I had experienced something that I was told was 'God' that had changed my life and I wanted to follow it wherever it would lead me. That has always been my disposition – one of trusting and following the nudges, tugs, and calls of the untamable Spirit of God onto every path that it revealed and through every door that it opened. As I have journeyed, like Abraham, from town to town and city to city, not knowing where I was going, but continually seeing God move in miraculous ways along the way. Sometimes, I have ended up in really unfortunate and unhealthy seasons and situations, and God has been faithful to lead me through those valleys onto the banks of the still, flowing streams. Other times, I have ended up in places where I have stood in awe of the wonder and magnificence of God. Sometimes, he has taken me out to gaze upon the night skies, like Abraham, and shown me the mysteries of life and existence.

Every step in this journey called life is gently guided by the subtle breeze of God's breath, bringing me into fresh, unexplored territories that I have never even dreamed of. I don't know where I am headed and I certainly don't know where I'll end up, but I am confident that as I remain open to the leading of my Father, he will lead me into the land flowing with milk and honey, wherever that may be. Even at this early stage in life, one thing that I have become absolutely confident of is that life is not about achieving goals, gaining notoriety, or reaching a destination. It is about the journey. To be a follower of Jesus is to commit to being a nomad, wandering the vast landscapes of life and eternity, never completely sure where you're at or where you're heading, but completely trusting that if Jesus is the one leading, everything is going to be just fine.

If you notice, the whole narrative arc of Scripture is about journey, wandering, and exodus, and almost never about arriving. It seems that almost every faithful follower of God throughout the Scriptures either never ended up at their destination or never had the opportunity to settle in to it. After wandering in the desert for 40 years, Moses saw the promised land from afar, but was never permitted to enter it. Jesus himself spoke of a Kingdom that he was sent to establish, but never saw the full realisation of it consummated on earth. The Apostle Paul continually spoke of running the race of life, straining towards the goal which was still far off. If none of these great spiritual leaders ever 'arrived', why have we spent so much time and energy trying to figure out how to take a short cut to get to the promised land? It seems to me that God has always been more interested in faithfulness to his leading and direction, wherever it may take us, than about reaching a place of certainty and comprehension.

I think the stories of Abraham, Moses, Jesus, Paul, and so many other spiritual leaders throughout history are meant to show us how vital it is for us to value each step along this journey of spirituality. The fact is, we're never going to 'arrive'. None of us is ever going to gain the certainty about life's complex mysteries that we so often long for. None of us is ever going to come close to figuring all of this out. And thank God! Because that's not the point. The point of our life is to grow in relationship and trust in the Lord as he continually calls us from one season to the next. To be willing to go wherever he leads, no matter what the cost. It's about searching for and relentlessly pursuing the God 'in whom we live, and move, and have our being'. (Acts 17:28) It's about gazing up in awe at the magnificent work of the creator that surrounds us at every moment of every day. It's about digging deep into our traditions and learning about our histories and heritage in order to understand how we ended up where we are today. It's about loving life, and everyone that journeys on this road alongside of us, honouring their journeys and marvelling at the diverse ways that God is drawing them along the path. It's about embracing and being grateful for our own unique journey and looking forward in hopeful anticipation and expectation for where God will lead us next.

Life is about the journey. We're all called to be nomads. God's Spirit continually is tugging on each of our hearts and beckoning us to take the next step forward into the unknown in full faith that God is with us, for us, and guiding us. None of us knows where exactly all of this is heading, but that's totally okay. Because the One who is sustaining all of it loves us deeply. And it's in the knowing that reality that we are freed to press forward onto new horizons, expectantly awaiting the next stop God has for us. It's not about the destination.

As I come to the end of this book, I feel like I am only at the very beginning. Though my short faith journey may have consisted of more twists and turns than the average person my age, it's not at all unique. No matter who you are, where you're at in life, or what you believe about God, we're all hungry for something more. We all yearn for meaning and purpose. And we will all spend our lives wandering around the plains of existence searching for the answers to satisfy our deepest longings. Some will find a place of contentment in a church or tradition. Others will find their home among the cynics and sceptics. Both of these are fine and needed options. But then there are the people like me, those who live for the feeling of the wind at our backs, gently pushing us forward on to the next experience with God as we seek to know him better. We, like Abraham, know that we may never see our promised land, but we refuse to give up the search.

Though I have come to realise that there is almost nothing I know with certainty, I can honestly say this: I *know* God. And not in the sense that I have knowledge about who God is or what he is like. No, I am certain that I have a deep experiential connection to the Creator of the universe. I have seen the hands of the Divine orchestrating my life with such beauty and creativity that it regularly leaves me standing in amazement. I have tasted of his Love, received his amazing grace, and communed deeply with the One who has created me. The grand Architect and Storyteller of the universe is the same One who lights my path. As the writer of the Proverbs notes, if we 'trust in the LORD with all of our hearts and rely not on our own understanding ... God will guide our paths.' (Proverbs 3:5-6 *paraphrase*) And I know this to be true. I see it every single day of my life. It is this reality that gives me hope, confidence, and courage to continue pressing ahead. I don't know what's around the next turn but I know that if I keep my ear attuned to the soft, still wind of God's Spirit, I will be gently pulled in the right path.

It is with this invitation that I leave you. Take the leap. Pack your bags and embark upon the journey that your soul is longing for. You may never know where it is that you're headed, and that's okay. Because the One who guides you is good. The world that lies just behind the boundaries of your comfort zone is brimming with creativity, life, and new experiences to be had.

Let the journey begin.

15

Wonder

'Our goal should be to live life in radical amazement...
[For] to be spiritual is to be **amazed**.'

Rabbi Abraham Joshua Heschel

As I stood on the edge of Lake Michigan, looking out over what seemed to be a never-ending body of water, tears formed in my eyes. The lights of the city glittered in the distance and the deep purple skies began to melt into the horizon. As the gentle breeze wafted across the lake and surrounded me, I couldn't shake the feeling that I was surrounded by the very presence of God. The turmoil and anxieties of my life lay just behind me in the city, but in this moment, I stood, breathed on by the Spirit of God that whispered silently to my soul, 'All is well.' This moment was a work of Divine art, painted by the very hands that formed my soul. This moment was all that I needed to know that everything was going to be okay. I didn't know what awaited me the next day, next week, or next year, but that didn't matter. Being concerned about the 'rightness' of my beliefs in this moment seemed laughable, because what words could I ever formulate that would describe what I was experiencing in this moment, on this beach? This simple, ordinary moment was all that it took to fill my soul and restore a deep peace to my heart. This moment was all that I had. And it was more than enough.

If I have learned anything so far in my short journey of faith it is this: that in every circumstance or situation, there is a vast untapped beauty lying just beneath the surface. And I believe that beauty is what we call God. Divine beauty isn't flashy or ostentatious. Instead, it is raw. It is simple. It is modest. When we live our lives with our eyes wide open, looking for God's presence in each and every moment, good or bad, we will live lives of peace. Lives filled with purpose. Lives filled with *wonder*.

That's what it means to be a Christian, after all. Beyond all of our theology, traditions, and practices, to be a Christian means to live every moment consciously aware that 'in God we live, and move, and have our being'. (Acts 17:28a) This is the message Jesus came proclaiming when he said, 'the Kingdom of God is in your midst!' The Kingdom is nothing more than the world waking up to the reality that God is our Source, the animator of all that is, seen and unseen. When Jesus calls for us to be 'born-again' it is so that we can 'see the Kingdom of God' (John 3:3), or to become aware of the presence of God in and around us at every moment of every day. When we are awakened to this reality, *everything* changes. The way we treat our neighbours, our friends, and even our enemies is fundamentally transformed because we understand that they too exist in the presence of God. As Paul says, 'we're [all] his offspring.' (Acts 17:28b) If Christ is the force that holds everything together (Colossians 1:17), then *everything* that exists is *sacred*. Every moment is holy. Every second is pulsating with Divine elegance. What would our lives be like if we actually believed all of that? How would we live? How would we face trials, challenges, and pain? When we recognise the beauty of God and the beauty of everything else, we cannot help but live with praise on our lips and joy in our hearts.

Spiritual nomads in every religion seem to have come to this one fundamental realisation – that the way to true and abundant life is to learn to live one's life in *wonder*.

Have you ever met someone who overflowed with the Spirit of God? People who come into proximity with you and you can just tell that there is something very different about them? Something that draws you to them and fills you with life. These people are the ones who live awestruck lives, constantly aware of the loving presence of their God. These people have wandered through the dry deserts and dark nights of the soul and have discovered that through it all, there is nothing left to fear. God is with them and everything is going to be okay.

During my junior year in college, as my blog and podcast began to take off, I was given the opportunity to interview one of the most influential mystics living today, Father Richard Rohr. I had heard a lot about him as I spent time exploring contemplative Christianity, but had never actually watched or listened to any of his teachings. I really had no clue what to expect. My co-host Troy and I arrived at his hotel early to set up our recording equipment and to go over the questions we had drafted for the interview. Both of us were noticeably nervous, totally unsure of what was about to unfold. As Father Rohr entered the room, a tangible sense of warmth came from him. As he sat down at our table and began conversing with us, the humility, joy, and peace that emanated from him literally brought tears to my eyes almost immediately. I don't mean to exaggerate the experience, but what was so incredibly moving was that it was so abundantly clear that Father Rohr *knew* God. That he was filled with God and constantly lived aware of the vastness and greatness of his Creator.

For the next hour as we sat and talked, my soul was moved. I knew that I too had a relationship with God, but in reality, my spiritual life was still more wrapped up in knowing about God than being aware of God's presence in and through all things. But what Father Rohr demonstrated, not only with his words but also with his being, was the power of living in wonder of God. He showed what one's life could look like if we moved from a place of religion to faith, from certainty to mystery, from expectation to awe. And to me, it looked a lot like Jesus. It looked like spirituality beyond the boundaries of religious institutions, doctrinal statements, and political positions. It looked really radical and so very simple all at the same time. After our interview had concluded, I stood and bear hugged him. I thanked him not for his time or even for the interview, but for his presence. For allowing himself to be a container, filled with the peace of God. For teaching me what it looked like to be a disciple of Jesus before he had even spoken a word. Before he we parted ways, I asked him how I could also get to a place of wonder and peace. 'Be patient and courageous. Seek experiences with God and always remain open and receptive to what you may find.'

Patience. Courage. Experience. Open. Find.

All words that had continually been appearing on my journey from fundamentalism to wherever I was heading now. It all seemed to be pointing me forward. Deeper into wandering. Deeper into uncertainty. Deeper into *God*. On the surface, none of this seemed to make much logical sense. How could these things bring me peace? How could my spiritual life possibly be enriched by living in constant unknowing and tension? And yet, the more I loosened my grip on everything that I had been taught to grasp so tightly to, the more light and peace began to shine through the cracks in this earthen vessel. The more of God I began to see and sense all around me. The more life began to well up within me.

It takes a lot of discipline to get to a place of wonder. Our lives are filled with distractions that call us away from reality and into our all-too-real imaginary worlds, filled with stress, worry, confusion, and cheap substitutes for what Jesus called 'the water of life'. Many of us live our lives unaware of the glory that surrounds us and pulsates through us each and every moment of the day. Instead, our focus is drawn to everything other than the fact that in this moment, God is here, life is beautiful, and there is hope.

It has been nearly two years since my conversation with Richard Rohr and five years since the start of this transformation of my faith, and I am still a long way from wholeness. In fact, over the last few years, I have become all the more aware of just how undisciplined, dysfunctional, unhealthy, and unkempt my life actually is. I struggle to make time for what matters most. I starve my soul of connection to God and find myself more committed to 'the desires of the flesh' than to the Kingdom of God. I still yearn for answers and lack fulfilment. I am all too aware of how far I still have to go before I could ever claim to have arrived at a place of 'enlightenment'.

But I am making progress. I am committed to wondering while I wander. I am committed to living out Father Rohr's advice, which actually originates from the lips of Jesus. I am committed to looking for God everywhere. I am committed to remaining open. I am committed to being patient. I am committed to casting aside my fears and embracing the journey. I may struggle to always live this out, but I am none the less committed. Because if there is anything that I have experienced to be true it is this: There is a God who is the Creator and Sustainer of Reality, he is Love, and because of that, in the end, everything is going to be okay. And when I remember those basic truths, wonder is unleashed. The ability to live with courage and to explore without pause, searching to find the next place where God is working in fresh and unexpected ways. In those moments where I find myself staring out over Lake Michigan, or looking up into the endless star-filled night sky, I remember these things and I wonder. When I find myself bent over in laughter with friends at the bar or am sitting across the table having an intimate conversation with someone I love, I get lost in the wonder of it all. In those dark nights where I lie in bed, wondering what the purpose of all of this is, I am lifted up and saved by wonder.

For me, wonder is synonymous with worship. When I am speaking of wonder, I am speaking of the deep resonance within that causes goosebumps to form on the skin and tears to well up in our eyes. I am speaking of that overwhelming sense of Love that washes over us when we think, read, speak, or sing words that attempt to express the majesty of God. We get to a place of wonder when we shift our thinking away from ourselves and our finiteness to the bigger picture, the larger narrative in which we find ourselves. We enter into wonder when we are humble enough to admit that we know nothing, but that there is *so* much to know. Wonder comes when we still our thoughts and our concerns and sit still in the moment in which we find ourselves. In the silence, we may hear the low hum of God's Spirit reverberating throughout the Universe. The only way we can live a life of wonder is when our impulse for certainty comes to an end and we embrace Truth, not as a claim, but as a person, a relational force, that is always with, and in, and through, and around us.

Wonder is the antidote to religion. Religion leads us to submission to systems and institutions. Religion leads us to be focused on 'fixing' our flaws and failures from the inside out. Religion is about power, wealth, and domination. Wonder, on the other hand, leads us to wandering. To liberating. To run free on the highways and byways of our lives. Wonder causes transformation, for when we sit in awe of the holiness of the Divine, we cannot help but be transformed and transfigured. Wonder reminds us of our powerlessness to change ourselves and the world on our own, yet fans the flames of the Spirit within and empowers us with a Divine force that can accomplish the impossible.

This is the goal for which I strive. This is the desire for which I long. For myself, for you, and for the entire world. That we would live lives of wonder, totally amazed at the goodness of God, the complexity of life, the diversity of human experience, and the peculiar reality that it all fits together somehow on to the giant canvas of the cosmos on which God is painting a beautiful masterpiece that defies comprehension. I know that I've got a way to go before I reach a place where my humility outweighs my desire to be right and my own issues seem less interesting than the life pulsating around me. But I will press on, because the journey is worth it. I will continue to wander, seeking for God wherever he is to be found. Patiently. Courageously. With Openness. Until wonder is found again. I hope you'll join me. Because when we all experience wonder together, I believe we will finally see God's Kingdom come and his will being done on earth as it is in heaven. *Amen.*

Acknowledgements

Writing and publishing this book has been quite the journey. I have felt the sting of rejection, grown tremendously, and discovered a far-spread family of amazing people who have encouraged me and guided me along the way.

To my extraordinary literary agent, Kathy Helmers, who has never stopped encouraging me, pushing me, and looking out for me since the day we shook hands in Nashville. I am so appreciative of you!

To David Moloney, Helen Porter, Will Parkes, and the whole team at Darton, Longman, Todd - thank you all for believing in this book and helping to redeem its journey! You all are absolutely wonderful.

To David Hayward who first connected me to DLT in the weeks following the cancelation of my book contract with Destiny Image - this simply could not have happened without you! Thanks!

To the many mentors and guides who have spoken into my life throughout the course of the birthing of this book: David Anderson, Brian McLaren, Laura Truax, Sharon Groves, Rob Bell, Mark Scandrette, Michael Kimpan, David Key, Danny Cortez, Stan Mitchell, Mark Tidd, Jenny Morgan, Vicky Beeching, David Rim, Kevin Lum, Reba Riley, Karl Wheeler, and Aaron Niequist. Your lives and witness inspire me to press on in this crazy journey! This book is a reflection of each one of your impacts on my life!

Acknowledgements

To my friends and loved ones who have offered so much support and encouragement to me throughout the years: Isaac Archuleta, Garrett Schlichte, Troy Medlin, Jonas Ganz, Kyle Stanton, Zach Spoerl, Kathryn Morgan, Will Eastham, Jeremiah Stanley, Quinton Bobb. You all are superstars.

To my mom, dad, brother, sister-in-law, and my beautiful niece and nephews: Brooklyn, Mason, Jordan, and Bentley. Thank you for always believing in me!

And finally, to the grand, beautiful, extraordinary mystery that I have come to know as Christ. May this book point many people to the abundant life we were always meant to experience and may God be glorified in it all!

About the author

Brandan Robertson is a noted Christian thought-leader, humanitarian, and commentator, working at the intersections of spirituality, sexuality, and social renewal.

Brandan writes regularly for *Patheos*, *Sojourners*, and *The Huffington Post*. He has published dozens of articles in respected outlets such as *TIME*, *The Washington Post*, *Religion News Service*, and *Dallas Morning News*. As a sought-out commentator on faith, culture, and public life, he is a regular contributor to national media outlets and has been interviewed by outlets such as *MSNBC*, *NPR*, *SiriusXM*, *TIME Magazine*, *The Wall Street Journal*, *The New York Times*, and *The Associated Press*.

Acclaimed as one of '*the most hope-inspiring young Christian leaders*', Brandan is a sought-after speaker and consultant to churches, denominations, conferences, and universities. He is the founder and executive director of *Nomad Partnerships*, a non-profit that equips and empowers people of faith to be fierce advocates for human rights. He served as the immediate past national spokesperson of *Evangelicals for Marriage Equality* and now serves on the advisory board. He is also on the editorial advisory board of *Stand Magazine* and on the board of initiators for *Convergence*.

Brandan earned his Bachelors Degree in Pastoral Ministry & Theology from Moody Bible Institute and is pursuing his Masters

About the author

of Theological Studies from Iliff School of Theology. He currently resides in Denver, Colorado.